street   ?

Blow Ye Winds Westerly

The Seaports & Sailing Ships
of Old New England

By the Author

HUCKLEBERRY HILL
*Child Life
in Old New England*

BLOW YE WINDS WESTERLY
*The Seaports & Sailing Ships
of Old New England*

Blow Ye Winds Westerly

THE SEAPORTS & SAILING SHIPS
OF OLD NEW ENGLAND

By Elizabeth Gemming

ILLUSTRATED

THOMAS Y. CROWELL COMPANY · NEW YORK

Contents

Acknowledgments

THE illustration on the title page is "Eastern View of Plymouth" by John Warner Barber, reproduced by courtesy of the Society for the Preservation of New England Antiquities.

The pictures on pages vi, 1, 20, 34, 61, 69, 75, 81, 98, 111, 112, 115, 136-137, and 161 were done by Albert Alden (1812–83), a designer and publisher of maps and engravings. The author is very grateful to Alden P. Johnson for permission to reproduce these illustrations from a proof book in his possession.

The whale's teeth (scrimshaw) on pages 101 and 171 are reproduced by permission of the National Gallery of Art, Index of American Design.

The memorial tablet quoted on page 105 is reprinted by permission of the Old Dartmouth Historical Society in New Bedford.

The 1851 Whale Chart on pages 124–125 appears through the courtesy of the United States Naval Oceanographic Office. The drawings of spouting sperm whales and right whales indicated the likely whereabouts of the huge mammals in each season, as spotted and reported by American mariners. (During the heyday of Pacific whaling, before the publication of this official chart, whalemen had tended to guard their personal knowledge of the best whaling grounds very jealously indeed.)

Permission to reproduce the whale-stamp impression on page 135 and the illustrated tally of whales on page 149 was granted by Stuart C. Sherman, author of *The Voice of the Whaleman*, and by its publisher, the Providence Public

Library. The tally records the whales taken by each whale-boat on a voyage of the bark *Smyrna* in 1853–57.

The author thanks James D. Mahoney for the use of his copy of *The Fisherman's Memorial and Record Book, containing A List of Vessels and Their Crews, Lost from the Port of Glouces-ter from the Year 1830 to October 1, 1873*. The advertisements on pages 84 and 99 are from this interesting volume, as are several anecdotes in the chapters on fishing.

Special thanks go to E. Harold Hugo for his excellent advice and assistance in assembling many of the illustrations in this book.

The author owes a particular "debt of inspiration" to the great American writer Herman Melville, above all for *Moby Dick*.

I

Yankee Land
and the Seven Seas

Farewell and adieu to you, Spanish ladies,
Farewell and adieu to you ladies of Spain,
Our captain's commanded we sail for New England
But we hope in a short time to see you again!

Importer's sign.
National Gallery of Art,
Index of American Design.

Old Salem, 1790-1812

A FRESH SPRING BREEZE was blowing in off the sea, and the brisk air smelled of salt and tar and spices. For half a mile along the waterfront, cobblestoned Derby Street ran through the heart of old Salem. Against a backdrop of spars, masts, rigging, and furled sails the wharves of the busy little seaport stretched like slender fingers straight out into the harbor. Open to ships on one side, the wharves were lined with warehouses, ironworks, sail lofts, ropewalks, counting rooms of merchant shipowners, apothecary shops, and ship chandleries well stocked with foodstuffs, rum, tobacco, boots, clothing, blankets, lanterns, hardware, oil, oakum, navigational instruments, logbooks, and a hundred other things.

Facing the wharves and close to the street stood the elegant mansions of the wealthy merchants. Not far away, dozens of wooden houses huddled together—small buildings blackened with age, with tiny-paned windows, overhanging second stories, and sharply pointed gables in the style of medieval England.

In the ironworks, the shipsmiths, dressed in leather aprons, were heating pieces of iron over roaring fires as apprentice boys tended the huge hand bellows overhead. Their hammers rang on the anvils as they shaped the iron into chains, cask hoops, anchors, and tools, and the red-hot metal hissed furiously as the smiths plunged it into cold water to temper and toughen it.

The sailmakers sat cross-legged in the sail lofts making new sails and mending old ones. After measuring the masts and yards of a ship, they sketched the sail patterns with chalk on the smooth wide floor, laid out the canvas, and cut

"Crowninshield's Wharf" by George Ropes.
Courtesy of the Peabody Museum of Salem.

it to size. Canvas ditty bags hung from the sailmakers' low benches, holding needles, hooks, twine, mallets, beeswax, and other gear. The sailmakers all wore protective leather "palms" strapped around their right hands, fitted with iron thimbles where they braced the eyes of their three-sided sail needles.

In the "ropewalks," low buildings several hundred feet long, hemp fibers were cleaned and straightened by being pulled through rows of iron spikes. Then a spinner coiled the fibers around his waist and walked away backwards, drawing the fibers taut, while a boy at a wheel twisted the ends round and round into "yarn." The yarns were rolled

up, tarred, rewound on bobbins, and stacked on a rack to season. Afterward they were threaded through the holes in a round metal plate, pulled through a tube, and twisted into "strands." Finally, in the far end of the ropewalk, three or more strands were parted out full length and tightly twisted into rope.

Nearby, the riggers were splicing ropes at their benches and going aloft in "bosun's chairs"—squares or crosses of wood that hung on ropes—to install the ropes, blocks, tackle, pulleys, and chains that would support the heavy masts and sails and yards and booms, as well as raise and lower all the complicated shipboard mechanisms.

Drays clattered back and forth over the cobblestones, trundling cargo to and from vessels at the wharves. Suddenly the air sparkled with the music of fife and drum, and around the head of the wharf marched a band of men from the ropewalk with cordage for a brand-new ship.

Jaunty sailors ambled around with their peculiar rolling walk. One sailor, his face as bronzed as an Indian's and his black hair long about his ears, called out to passersby, trying to sell the grumpy lime-green parrot that sat on his shoulder. Ragged little boys gaped at the tattooed forearms of the seamen and hung around the boardinghouses and dance halls in the alleys to hear the men joking and cursing in a dozen different languages.

Salem boys—and girls too—loved the wharves. They haunted the shipyards, standing timidly among the tools and wood chips to watch the carpenters and wood-carvers. They tried not to get in the workmen's way, and hoped to be asked to hold an axe or a tar bucket for a moment.

In the winter ox teams had hauled in great loads of oak and pine by sled to Salem, as well as to Newburyport, Medford, and all the other shipbuilding towns on the Merrimack, Mystic, and North rivers of Massachusetts. Tall mast pines from the inland forests awaited the start of spring shipbuilding. Now the shipyards echoed with the sounds of pounding and the bold voices of the men singing their work songs, and with the cry of "Grog oh!" at eleven and at four that signaled breaks in the day's labor.

The friendliest of the shipyard workers were the ship wood-carvers who made the figureheads to be placed on the bows of the vessels for identification. These figureheads pictured generals and statesmen (especially George Washington), Indian chiefs and princesses, and ladies in white

Figurehead,
"Twin Sisters."
*From the collections of the
Marine Historical Association,
Inc., Mystic, Connecticut.*

gowns (white for luck, and never black). Some portrayed
the wives and daughters of shipowners and captains, and
even these men themselves. Seaport children often sneaked
into the shipyards and posed for the wood-carvers.

Some figureheads were elaborate, with parts that could
be unscrewed at will. One day out of port, a vessel would
"heave to" while the crew removed the figurehead and
packed it carefully away in the hold. It would be put back
in place whenever the vessel neared a port. Sailors were extremely superstitious about figureheads. They believed that
a damaged figurehead foretold woe to the voyage, and a
figurehead lost in a gale meant certain doom. (One captain
was able to put down a mutiny by stealing to the bow with

a bucket of black paint and threatening to paint the white-gowned figurehead the color of disaster.)

Old Salem was a city of great wealth between the Revolutionary War and the War of 1812, yet it had a population of only about eight thousand people. Several merchants amassed fortunes of more than a million dollars, a fabulous sum of money in those days. They owned or chartered ships to distribute their cargoes, but they were not shopkeepers themselves. The East India merchants of Salem were people with excellent taste, and they used their fortunes to build fine houses in a new style: square houses of wood or brick with three stories, white picket fences with beautifully carved gateposts, and pleasant gardens and lovely walks out back.

The oldest brick house in town stood at the head of Derby Wharf. Its main staircase had a rail so finely carved that each upright formed a different spiral. The interior of the house was paneled in wood, painted in soft pastel colors, and decorated with fine "tea-chest" wallpaper.

Around 1800, however, the well-to-do folk of Salem began to move away from the bustling waterfront. Their newer mansions lined Essex and Chestnut streets—square brick homes with arched doorways that were framed with sidelights and crescent fanlights, and elegant porches flanked by columns with carved capitals. Rows of shade trees marched along the wide avenues. Formal gardens were laid out behind the houses, and even the stables were carefully designed to make a generally pleasing effect.

There were usually four spacious rooms to a floor, furnished with rare teakwood furniture and exquisite porcelains, selected in China by young Salem captains and officers and carried home halfway around the globe in the holds of

Salem ships. The finest chairs and tables had been carved by entire families of Chinese wood-carvers, who spent their lifetime on a single piece. Bowls of carved soapstone rested on tiny teak stands, and screens of embroidered silk were atangle with entwined serpent and animal designs.

Salem housewives prized their Cantonware so highly that they cared for it themselves, no matter how many servants they had. In white aprons they sat before cedar washtubs while their maids brought hot water, soap in a dish, and soft linen towels, and they washed, rinsed, and dried one precious plate, cup, and bowl after another.

Salem people loved flowers—in fact, most New Englanders did. The gardens of the seaport towns had China asters among the beds of snapdragons, roses, day lilies, peonies, and geraniums, all set apart by charming paths. Wherever there was space for them, there were fruit trees—apple, pear, peach, cherry, plum, and quince—and lilac bushes and honeysuckle framed the doorways. Out in back, in the kitchen gardens, herbs and berries and small vegetables grew, and larger plots were filled with beans, squash, potatoes, and turnips. And on sunny south slopes, peas, cucumbers, and melons spread out in a pretty tumble of rich green vines.

Salem folk preferred a rather simple social life, for they disliked waste and idle showiness. They had won their fortunes at sea and in distant lands through bravery, skill, and plain hard work, and so they did not mind working with their hands, indoors and out. They rose early, at six in summer and seven thirty in winter, and managed to keep busy all day. Their favorite time was the twilight hour before the lamps were lit. It was an hour for quiet reflection after the day's work was done, and they encouraged their children to make good use of it. The whole family would enjoy a peaceful "sit" or a stroll in the fenced back garden among the hollyhocks and bluebells, past the sundial and out to the little summerhouse at the far end.

After six-o'clock "tea" (supper) there was more busy work, such as mending, but later there was often a little time for games, and the boys went out to call on their friends.

The mistresses of the Salem mansions were excellent cooks. They worked along with the servants at canning and preserving, and they made their own pies. Every Saturday the brick ovens were filled with the week's supply of pies, breads, cakes, cookies, and baked beans in pots. Saturday was also housecleaning day because everything had to be sparkling clean for the Sabbath, when no work was done at all.

No girl was considered worth marrying until she was an accomplished cook, and the family servants took great pride in teaching the daughters of the house all their kitchen secrets. Once a girl was out of school—by her early teens— she was expected to preside graciously at the tea table and help her mother entertain.

Town merchants and their families, like the country people, enjoyed a nice carriage drive or a sleigh ride. In winter, large sleighs went from house to house to pick up twenty or thirty invited guests and drove on to a village tavern for dancing and a late supper. A fishing party in the bay was a favorite summer excursion, and so was a picnic sail to a nearby island to stroll and sing and feast on chowder cooked in an iron pot over a driftwood fire.

The Salem mansions had rooms large enough to hold forty or fifty people, for there were lots of evening parties. Schoolchildren delivered the invitations on their way to

classes. The parties were quite informal. The ladies brought
their fine sewing and embroidery, and all the guests sat in
one big circle to chat and to drink tea or coffee with biscuits, pound cake, fruit whip, and perhaps a light wine.

Quite a few of Salem's lovely carved doorways were decorated with pineapple designs, the ancient symbol of hospi-
tality. One sea captain's wife had a wooden pineapple set up
over her front door that was so tall it almost reached the
middle of the center second-story window. The blinds had
to be cut away so that they could be shut around it. Every
year the proud lady had the pineapple freshly gilded, and
it shone as brightly as the polished brass door knocker
below.

Salem parents were unusually devoted to their children,
and one year a group of wealthy fathers decided to organize
a series of dances for their sons and daughters. The first
"assembly" was held just after Christmas, with six dances
a season, at five thirty in the afternoon. Partners for the
opening dances were always drawn by lot. Black fiddlers

Pineapple,
by an unknown artist.
Abby Aldrich Rockefeller
Folk Art Collection,
Williamsburg, Virginia.

played on and on through countless merry polkas and reels. Parents attended too. In fact, some of the older gentlemen were the most graceful of all. They would jump high and cross their feet, and they took care never to slide as they performed the intricate steps of the dances.

The ladies wore pearls and gold bangles with their exquisite gowns, which had been made to order from China silk. The frocks of the young belles were of silk or Indian cotton. Though the dresses were fashioned of the richest plum, white, yellow, and print fabrics imported in family ships, the styles were simple. On their way to the party, the younger girls covered their hair with little hoods or, in winter, fur caps frilled with lace, tied under their chins in bows. The older women had gossamer camel's-hair shawls from Arabia, shawls so delicate they could be drawn through a wedding ring. The shawls were white in the center and bordered with palm leaves embroidered in blue and black, and they were so costly that each was identified by a number in case of loss. The ladies wore the lovely shawls over their shoulders and draped over one arm.

After hours of dancing, a supper was served at ten. It was a hearty and elegant meal of roast turkey and duck, ham, hot and cold tongue, pies, tarts, cakes, and wine. These suppers were supplied by one of Salem's most popular caterers, a prosperous black man who was famous for the excellent turtle soup he advertised in the newspaper at fifty cents a quart.

Ship launchings were regular gala events in the old seafaring town. Banks of seats were set up and sold to spectators for a quarter apiece. Thousands of people crossed the causeway to Winter Island or thronged to Naugus Head, or even watched from boats. Whenever a new vessel slid down

"Salem Common on Training Day, 1808" by George Ropes.
Courtesy, Essex Institute, Salem, Massachusetts.

the tallow-greased ways into the sea, the citizens cheered with joy and pride.

Animal and magician shows occasionally came to town, and although they were denounced by the clergy, they were thoroughly enjoyed by the townsfolk. Several Salem ships brought exotic animals home—an African lion, a camel, an elephant—and the creatures were exhibited before large and curious crowds. When a Salem bark arrived with a pair of rare Arabian stallions, a present from the sultan to a Salem merchant, there was a private horse show. Bare-legged grooms dressed in turbans, colorful robes, and sandals tended the beautiful horses, for the animals understood only Arabic commands.

The militia muster or training day was always the best show of all. The Boston Brass Band arrived by stagecoach after having been cheered at every stop along the way. There were Punch and Judy shows, fife-and-drum music, and plenty of gingerbread and punch to devour. Militia companies from all the surrounding towns marched through the streets of Salem to the common, followed by a gay mob of spectators.

The patriotic people of the town supported their militia companies enthusiastically, and the corps was always full. There were four divisions: artillery, grenadiers, light infantry, and riflemen. There was quite a bit of friendly rivalry over uniforms. The Salem Cadets, who came from the most prominent families, wore scarlet coats, white waistcoats, ruffled shirts, white breeches, stockings fastened at the knee with black garters, and cocked hats with plumes atop their powdered hair. The Salem Light Infantrymen wore blue coats with scarlet linings and brass buttons and lots of gold lace, white waistcoats, breeches seamed with scarlet, and brass helmets with bright red horsehair plumes that swooped stylishly down to the right.

But holidays were rare, and most days were school days. Many well-to-do children started school at the age of two or three. They went to private "dame schools" run by impoverished spinsters of good family in their own homes. Babies were put on the waiting lists of the better dame schools as soon as they were born, and every child's family history was carefully checked before he was admitted.

Pupils were expected to learn reading, sewing, and good manners. In one school, kept upstairs in the teacher's house, the little scholars were sternly called to order by a tap of the pencil on the teacher's desk. Religious exercises came first, and later they read and spelled aloud, learned to count with wooden beads strung on a wire, and sang the multiplication tables to the tune of "Yankee Doodle." Anyone who misbehaved was punished by a sharp tap on the head with a thimble, and very bad children were made to stand in the closet among the coats.

The children made beaded bags and samplers from approved patterns, and the stitches were supposed to be all but invisible. The boys sewed too—sewing would be a most useful skill on board ship someday. (Quite a few sea captains hooked and braided rugs as a hobby at sea.)

A few days before the New Year, a special holiday at the dame schools, several pupils called on parents to collect money for the teacher. Then they wrapped up the money, and the pupil with the neatest handwriting addressed the packet. It was presented on New Year's Day with great ceremony while everyone crowded around to see. Of course, the teacher needed the money badly and expected it too, but she always pretended to be taken completely by surprise. She thanked the children graciously, and then each pupil received a gift from her—often a little jointed wooden doll, flat-footed and only about three inches tall, from a Salem "cent shop."

These penny shops were also run by poor gentlewomen who were forced to work for a living. The shops were usually in the small front rooms of mossy-roofed old houses. In some it was dark and mysterious, in others just peaceful and nice. A tiny shop bell tinkled whenever young customers opened the door and stepped shyly in onto the floor that had been strewn with fresh sand to keep it clean. Salem children were convinced that all the treasures of the Orient lurked somewhere within the cent shops.

Actually the shelves were lined with bolts of printed cotton for aprons and dresses, papers of buttons, needles and thread, bars of soap, and boxes of candles. There were sometimes barrels of flour, cornmeal, apples, beans, split peas, brown sugar, or biscuits. The glass cases in front held the little wooden dolls and all sorts of penny purchases—marbles, whistles, even raisins.

One copper cent, as big as a modern half dollar, was a small fortune to a child, and the boys and girls deliberated long and hard before exchanging their cents for something from the case. There was a tempting array of sweets that usually won them over in the end: sheets of paper with pink and white dropped peppermints in very precise rows, dancing "Jim Crows" of gingerbread, and gingerbread elephants and dromedaries to munch on the way to school or on the way home.

Salem candies, particularly the stony "Gibraltars," became world-famous in later years. They reposed in glass jars, and came in lemon or peppermint or checkerberry flavor, all neatly done up in white paper. Salem captains took them to sea to eat when they felt homesick, and Salem girls gave packages of Gibraltars and molasses "Black Jacks" to their seafaring sweethearts to remember them by.

When a returning ship was overdue, the townsfolk naturally worried about their husbands, fathers, brothers, sons, and friends. The merchants climbed the garret ladders and emerged on their rooftops to scan the horizon with their telescopes. Boys waited impatiently on the Neck or on Juniper Point, lying on their stomachs on the rocks and watching for sails. At the first sign of a mighty ship they raced back to Derby Wharf to spread the news. All the townspeople who could leave their work streamed down to the wharves, while the dame-school pupils wriggled in their seats and yearned to go there too.

The captains had special favorites among the children of the town, and they never failed to tuck away little presents for them—perhaps a rice-paper book or a carved ivory animal, a tiny chess set or a gold wishing ring. One boy got a suit of clothes of silk with gold lace trim, exactly like the suits worn by the sons of the noblemen of India. A Salem girl, just eight years old, received one perfect pearl from her captain friend, and each time he returned from a new voyage he brought her another until she had a priceless necklace.

Round the point, a great East Indiaman was coming into view! The ensign flew from the topmast, thank goodness, so the people on shore knew that no man had died during the voyage. The ship fired the salute; the salute was returned from the shore; and the crowd began to cheer.

On board, however, the captain, the officers, and the crew still waited anxiously, half afraid of some unknown tragic news that might await them on the dock. They had been away a year or longer, with little word from home. For one man, a beloved face would be missing. For another, luckier one, a new little face might be there—the baby born in his absence, tearful and suspicious of the stranger who would try to pick it up and hug it.

Frantic counting-room clerks, meanwhile, were hurrying to hire a gang of men to unload the cargo, and in the taverns and boardinghouses of the waterfront alleys the help was scurrying about to spruce the dingy places up for the sailors. Pet parrots squawked and pet monkeys jabbered, and everybody rushed back and forth to get the best view.

Minutes later, when the tall East Indiaman was in from

the Orient, the crowd quieted and made a path for the captain and officers to come ashore. A turbaned cabin boy from Calcutta followed the master at a respectful distance, glancing shyly to right and to left at the strange folk of Yankeeland.

Boston Town

IN COLONIAL DAYS Boston was known as "the market town of the West Indies," and its harbor was even busier than Salem's. The West Indies traders stored long rows of molasses casks on the wharves, and no boy could ever resist putting a stick into one of the open bungholes and licking off the molasses that stuck to it. Some was thin and sour, and some was thick and sweet—the best casks were already covered with drippings spilled by the boys who had been there first.

Boston had some eighteen thousand people right after the Revolutionary War. It grew so fast that by 1830 it numbered more than sixty thousand inhabitants. Dock Square was its shopping center, and nearby State Street was becoming the headquarters of the banks and the marine insurance firms. The business streets were paved with cobblestones from nearby beaches. Oystermen wheeled their wares up from the wharves, coopers' and sailmakers' apprentices rushed about, and peddlers hawked limes from wheelbarrows. Boston was a town of masts and church spires, fine bridges, and slate or mossy shingle rooftops, and the new State House with its gilded dome watched over the town from the top of Beacon Hill.

"The Old Warehouse, Dock Square" (also known as
"The Old Cocked Hat" and "The Old Feather Store").
Courtesy, The Bostonian Society, Old State House.

Some fifty brick stores ran a quarter of a mile down the middle of one of the built-up wharves. Three great auction halls for the sale of cargo occupied the upper story of the wharf complex, and an eight-sided cupola was the headquarters for a semaphore company that received signals from incoming ships. Counting-room clerks sat on high stools before open fireplaces, busily writing in leatherbound ledgers or rummaging in safes and chests that contained each vessel's business records. They could watch new ships being rigged through the small-paned office windows.

Boston originally occupied a small peninsula, almost an island, edged by mud flats and marshes and graced by three hills. Very early in its history the people began filling in some of the coves, but fingers of half-salty water still reached far into the heart of the town. Boys tried skating on the edges of these inlets in winter, and fished there for smelts for their breakfast in the spring. Pigeons hung around the sheds and stables on the Neck, where country farmers arrived with their wagonloads of foodstuffs. Hundreds of teams drew up in Haymarket Square, the bazaar where the city's official hay scales stood.

Boston was very much like a large country town, except that folks in Boston stayed up later at night. The wharves were busy around the clock. Bakers had barely begun their work by nine or ten in the evening, and were nowhere near done when the watchman clumped over the cobblestones crying, "One o'clock and a warm fair night, all's well!" Early in the morning the bakers' carts rattled through the streets, leaving hot rolls and loaves on doorsteps, and the milkmen with their cans went from door to door leaving pails of fresh white milk.

Boston folk went to "meeting" on the Sabbath, morning and afternoon, like all good Yankees, and did no unnecessary work that day. Fathers led family prayers morning and evening, and Sunday evening was specially reserved for visiting.

Lively, busy Boston grew and grew. A new town wharf was built for market boats. Commercial Street was laid out to the north past the heads of the wharves, while India and Broad streets edged the waterfront to the south. But the center of mercantile Boston remained the old State House, a small brick building that housed the entire city government, post office, a merchants' club and reading room, and a news bureau. People were so eager for news that every editor tried his best to print exclusive stories. Even on the Sabbath, editors hurriedly set extras for boys to hawk in the streets of the city. People rushed forward to buy the handbills that still smelled of fresh printer's ink. News bulletins were received by a system of signals relayed from ships by way of an island in the harbor. Reporters in charge of ship news hurried out by rowboat, competing to be the first to board an incoming vessel and so get their hands on every foreign paper the captain had with him. Some captains, forgetting they would be expected to arrive home with long-awaited bulletins, neglected to pick up the latest papers in foreign ports the day they sailed for New England. These captains, of course, were highly unpopular.

Boston was still a town built of wood in those days, and hardly a night went by without a fire somewhere in the city —in the North End, on the hills, on the wharves. The old-fashioned private fire societies, in which members were pledged to fight fires only at the homes of other members,

Family of Chimney Sweeps, from "Six Trades" by Nathaniel Dearborn. *Worcester Art Museum.*

"Boston from City Point" by W. J. Bennett.
M. & M. Karolik Collection. Courtesy, Museum of Fine Arts, Boston.

had given way to volunteer fire companies that served entire neighborhoods. Every Boston boy was certain that his
local engine company was the best in the world.

When a blaze broke out, everyone ran up and down the
street yelling "Fire!" There were no signals or alarm boxes,
but as soon as the churches could be opened, the church
bells of the town joined in giving the alarm. Each local engine company assembled and began to drag its engine by a
stout rope the moment enough men and boys had arrived
to pull it. Everybody made it his business to attend a fire,
in fact, and the noise of the engines and the shouts of the
mob were terrific.

Every good engine was a "suction engine," able to pump water either from a well or directly from the sea and to throw it to a great height. The first engine to arrive at the scene of the fire stationed itself by the source of water and began pumping, and the next and the next and the next took their places side by side, pumping the water through their hoses so that it could be turned on the flames.

The volunteer firemen, who received no pay and had no uniforms, were among the most energetic and public-spirited young men in town. The one wish of a young Boston lad was to reach eighteen and join his neighborhood fire company. Until that day, the least he could do was to follow the volunteers and scream "Fire!" at the top of his lungs, and hope to be allowed to help pull the rope dragging the engine.

Several busy railroad lines from inland terminated at the waterfront, and sailing packets were even busier distributing the goods that entered Boston from all corners of the world. Every tidewater village up and down the coast had its packet schooner or sloop connection to Boston, wind and weather permitting. As the city's population approached a hundred thousand during the 1840s, there was not enough land in the town for all the people, for the tidal flats of the Back Bay were not yet filled in. There was no city water supply (and no plumbing) until 1848. Pale-faced apprentice boys in coarse shirts and breeches took down shop shutters in the early morning dampness and trudged wearily to the neighborhood pumps for pails of water. Day laborers hurried by with tin lunch pails through the crooked streets of the dismal North End, a careworn district of sailors' boardinghouses and dingy dance halls, where half the population was foreign-born, mostly Irish. Aged men made the rounds begging for odd jobs, and scavenger pigs rooted in the narrow, rundown lanes.

The middle classes were moving out to the West End, South Boston, and East Boston. The most fashionable people settled in mansions or red brick town houses on Beacon Hill, once a wasteland of huckleberry bushes and cow pastures. Beacon Street became a stylish promenade shaded by magnificent elms, with blocks of fine brick houses on one side facing the Common. Many free black families lived in small wooden houses on the north slope of Beacon Hill.

Most people lived in Boston all the year round, for long-distance travel was roundabout and difficult. Town boys sat patiently on the rail of the bridge to Cambridge in summer, waiting to hook a flounder or two. People fortunate enough to own a carriage took drives in the countryside along wooded lanes, past pastures and sheep commons.

As early as 1818, a summer excursion to Nahant on the steamer was many a Boston child's introduction to the

Staffordshire plate,
"The Hotel at Nahant,"
by Joseph Stubbs.
Society for the Preservation of New England Antiquities.

"real ocean." The boys and girls from town loved the beaches, where they discovered horseshoe crabs, rays' egg cases, sea urchins, sand dollars, and endless varieties of pink-purple, leather-brown, and lettuce-green seaweeds.

The year-round center of activity for all Boston was the Common—a combination meadow, cow pasture, playground, and training ground for the militia. The cows stayed in the more remote corners of the area. The Common was enclosed by a double fence, inside and outside the malls for strolling, and the six-sided railings made excellent seats for watching a militia muster. Boston boys went "hoop driving" on the malls, with their prized large hoops from sea-going casks. They played marbles and flew their kites on the Common. There were only a couple of trees to get in the way of the kites, including a nice willow by the Frog Pond (which had small fish but, apparently, no frogs).

The townsfolk assembled on the Common on special occasions, such as musters, the two militia election days, and Independence Day. The city constable turned up to keep order—Boston had no uniformed police department until mid-century. Every man between the ages of eighteen and forty-five (unless exempt) was required to appear twice a year with his gun, belt, and cartridge box for inspection

Toy vendors,
from "Six Trades"
by Nathaniel Dearborn.
Worcester Art Museum.

Vendors of dolls and fruit,
from "Six Trades"
by Nathaniel Dearborn.
Worcester Art Museum.

and drill. The special volunteer companies in their snappy uniforms paraded more often.

Election Day, when the new officers were chosen, was held for many years on the last Wednesday in May. Every Boston child expected " 'Lection money"—perhaps a nine-pence—to spend on the Common, where vendors set up tables, tents, and stalls. Boys went with boys and girls went with girls to spend their money almost entirely on things to eat and drink. There were coconuts, pieces of sugar cane, dates, and tamarinds for sale, and large candy medals stamped with the head of the first governor of the Massachusetts Bay Colony and known as "John Endicotts." Sailors stood around devouring lobsters, while hungry youngsters gobbled up raw oysters, two for a cent, with salt and pepper and vinegar, under the trees of the Park Street mall. Men dispensed spruce beer and ginger beer from funny wheel-barrows decorated with pictures of bottles popping their corks. The drinks cost two cents a glass, but most of the vendors were willing to sell half a glass for one cent.

There was no long summer school vacation then—just one or two weeks in June and a couple of weeks in August, besides half holidays Thursdays and Saturdays. After sev-

"George Richardson" (son of a Boston wine merchant) by an unknown artist. *Private collection.*

eral years in a small private school, a qualified nine-year-old boy entered the old Latin school, for which he had to know a little arithmetic and be well grounded in spelling. Boys from all backgrounds attended the school, not just those from well-to-do homes. The morning bell rang at eight in the spring and summer and at nine in the fall and winter. It sounded for five minutes, and when it stopped, every boy had to be in his place. School let out at noon and resumed at three, and went on until six in summer and until dark in winter. There were no long recesses because there was hardly any play space anyway, and the boys spent most of the day sitting on long hard benches.

Latin school was a five-year course based on a single book: the Latin grammar. Since the aim of the school was to develop good memories, the boys memorized the whole grammar book in their first year! Saturday was the day for "declamations," and once a month each lad had to give a speech. The boys were placed in grades solely according to their knowledge of Latin, and so the arithmetic and English lessons were often a confusion of different levels.

It was not unheard of for bright boys to enter Harvard College at thirteen or fourteen. They took the entrance examinations, many of which were oral, from six in the morning until seven at night on one day, and from six until two the following day. Then they were free at last to loiter around the hall and wait for the president and the faculty members to call each one of them in turn and tell him whether or not he would be admitted.

Homesick Harvard freshmen had over an hour of prayers and recitations before a breakfast of coffee and milk, butter, cold bread, and a different hot bread each day. They had meat, potato, and "pudding" every day for dinner—beef or veal or mutton or meat pie or salt fish; rice, cornmeal mush, or Indian pudding, and pie once a week. The food was quite good. The boys pretended it wasn't, but it was.

After four long years of recitations, chapel, and study in the library, commencement signaled the end of boyhood.

On the morning of that day, even before daybreak, a procession of townspeople, many of them black, went from Boston to Cambridge, pushing small covered handcarts. They settled themselves around Cambridge common and offered food and drink to thirsty and hungry graduates, guests, and bystanders. Harvard's commencement was the year's biggest public holiday in Cambridge town.

Among the wealthy people of Boston, social life was quite formal. "Society" included wealthy professional men, important people in politics, shipowners, and merchants—the East Indies trade had so much prestige that the best compliment a pretty, well-bred girl could receive was, "She is good enough to marry an East India captain." The "best families" of Boston preferred the old-fashioned dress and manners of Colonial days, for most of them had been prominent in the town since well before the Revolution.

One typical merchant regularly ate a hearty breakfast each wintry day and then relaxed in his dressing gown of China silk while being shaved by his West Indian barber, who came by each morning and told the merchant all the latest gossip. Then the merchant dressed and left the house on foot, accompanied by a black servant. They walked to the markets near Faneuil Hall, where huge sleds from the country stood piled with butter and cheese, fresh and salt meat, carrots and turnips, and barrels of cider and "perry" (pear cider). Street urchins slyly sucked cider from the barrels through straws while the farmers were not looking. The merchant selected food for the day's dinner, and when he had made his choices, the servant carried them home in a basket. The merchant himself proceeded alone to his counting rooms on India Wharf. In winter, when the large ships were at sea, there was not really much to do at the office—

Butcher's sign. *National Gallery of Art,*
Index of American Design.

just a few accounts, and some future planning. The business
day was over by twelve thirty or one, and all the merchants
met for " 'Change," talking business and politics on the
sidewalk or, in bad weather, in some tavern or insurance
office.

Dinner was served at home about two thirty, with several
courses accompanied by punch and wines, and if there were
important guests, it might last until twilight. If no company
was present, the whole family then went out for a sleigh
ride in winter, or perhaps a drive in the country in summer
to take afternoon tea at a friend's house. In the evening the
merchant and his wife frequently attended a ball or a supper party; or they just sat down to a simple cold meal at
home.

Since Christmas was not celebrated in old New England,
the year's grandest holiday was Thanksgiving. Preparations
began at least three weeks before the day itself. Houses were
cleaned from top to bottom, and fresh bed canopies and

curtains hung. All the best china and glassware were carefully washed and dried, and the silver was polished until it
gleamed. The table linen was washed and bleached and

Silver teapot, by John Coney of Boston.
National Gallery of Art, Index of American Design.

freshly ironed, and even the kitchen floor and tables were
scrubbed white. And all kinds of pies were baked and
stored.

The whole family attended meeting on Thanksgiving
morning. The children were given coins to donate to the
collection that was traditionally taken for the poor. Back
home, done up in their very best clothes, the younger children waited for all their cousins to arrive and the merriment
to begin.

Dinner started at about two o'clock. A large table was
set up in the back parlor for the grown-ups, and a smaller
side table was nicely laid for the children. They tried to

outdo one another telling jokes and stories, and they sometimes whooped so loud that the elders had to get up from
their table and shush them. In some families the eldest son
helped his father carve the turkey. There was no soup and
no fish course, but never mind, the turkey was preceded by
chicken pie! The older people drank wine, and the children
had cider. Vegetables came with the turkey itself, and then
came the mince and squash and apple and lemon or Marl-
borough pies, the cranberry tarts, and the blazed plum
pudding with blue flames dancing lightly over its surface.
In at least one old New England family it was the custom
to place before each guest a plate filled with six wedges of
pie, each a different kind, to be taken home from the feast
and eaten later.

The banquet was so leisurely that the candles and lamps
had to be lighted by the time the raisins, dried figs, prunes,
dates, and walnuts were served. At last, the grown-ups
adjourned to the front parlor to go on talking about their
ancestors and the family business, while the children settled
down to old maid and jackstraws.

Nobody gave a thought to supper on Thanksgiving night!

North of Boston
and Down East to Maine

ALL UP AND DOWN the North American coast, from Nova
Scotia to New Orleans, two- and three-masted "coasters"
carried on a steady traffic. Yankee brigs, sloops, and schooners,
built and manned in the small seaports of northern Massachusetts, New Hampshire, and Maine, sailed forth laden

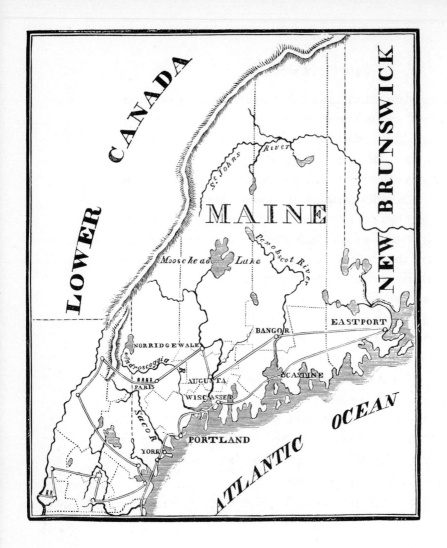

with the products of Yankee farms, forests, fisheries, and factories. They took apples and fish to Philadelphia or Norfolk and returned with cargoes of coal. Southerners ordered plain shoes and strong cotton cloth from the mills of Massachusetts and Rhode Island to clothe their slaves, and sent for granite for their public buildings. The coasters delivered their shipments and came back from Charleston and Savannah with cotton, corn, bacon, and hams. These busy coastal vessels, of course, also distributed the imported goods that arrived from overseas at the great port of Boston.

Numerous Maine towns, in particular, had long specialized in the building of fine ships. Portland, Camden, and Thomaston also traded directly with the West Indies. Castine, a base for smugglers during the War of 1812, shipped fish and timber to the islands in return for dyes and molasses. By 1840 the town of Bangor, on the great Penobscot River at the edge of the forest, had become North America's most important lumber-shipping center.

"Marblehead Counting House" by an unknown artist. *Private collection.*

"Fishing Houses in the Spring" by William P. ("Billy") Stubbs,
age 18. *Private collection.*

Pleasant Thomaston was a typical sprawling, lively
Maine-coast community that made its living receiving and
shipping goods by road and by water. The shore village of
Thomaston (now known as Rockland) was a distribution
center for Nova Scotia potatoes and salmon. Passenger
schooners arrived and departed almost every day, along
with freight brigs from Halifax, Portland, Boston, and Providence. Wind and weather conditions were a round-the-
clock concern—sleighing was miserable in blowing snow,
and the roads that were "hubbly" in winter turned to
"slush" in the spring. Even in summer, fierce gales blew in
off the sea, and salty fogs settled regularly down upon the
houses of the village like cold, soggy feather comforters.

Yet all the coastal towns were in close touch with the outside world, far more so than the farm villages of the back

country. The workaday routine went on all year round, but
there were many diversions. There were turkey and goose
shoots in November, just before Thanksgiving, when a
simple family dinner of a roast bird, plum pudding, and
wine was followed by a visit to the neighbors for some singing and dancing.

One winter evening the people of Thomaston enjoyed a
concert of sacred music, with a soloist from Boston, assisted
by the local choir. It was held in the meetinghouse promptly
at seven. Admission was twenty-five cents, although there
was a family ticket for a dollar that admitted six. Some
weeks later a traveling troupe of equestrians came with their
horses to perform at the town hotel before a crowd of five
hundred spectators.

Summer was the time for clamming parties and "rambles"
to look for strawberries, raspberries, and mushrooms. One
cherry-picking party consisted of twenty-six chaises that
proceeded together to the orchard of a generous neighbor.

"Home of Captain Oliver Lane"
by Alfred J. Wiggin. *Private collection.*

The girls and young men ate all the cherries they could hold and took home as many cherries as they could carry.

River cruises were popular, and so were fishing parties. One very nice fishing party set out from Thomaston for Owl's Head on a sunny day in July. The young men left their horses and chaises in the care of the lighthouse keeper and went out in small boats to fish. Later they picnicked, played ninepins, and rambled over the rock ledges with the girls.

Not every excursion was a success in the changeable weather of the rugged coast of northern New England, however. On one almost incredibly lovely summer morning a group of young people were well along on a twenty-four-mile sail from their Maine village straight out to sea, to Matinicus Rock to inspect the new lighthouse that was under construction. Abruptly the wind shifted, the gray water grew choppy, and nearly everyone got seasick. By the time they approached the rocky island, the sea was too rough to land their boat, so they had to turn around in the rain and head back to the mainland.

One of the most picturesque of the small old Yankee seaports was Portsmouth, on New Hampshire's short stretch of seacoast. From its sheltered harbor, vessels had carried on a thriving West Indies trade before the War of 1812. Shipsmiths had forged iron spikes and bolts near the wharves, while woodworkers shaped pine planks, oak oars, keels of elmwood, spruce spars, maple cabin-paneling, and towering masts from mighty white pine trunks. Gradually, then, all the smaller seaports grew quieter as foreign trade and shipbuilding activities began to center in Boston.

Years later, in the 1840s, retired merchants in old-fashioned high-collared coats strolled through the wide streets, possibly detecting an aroma of spices that seemed, to them, to linger in the air. Fine coaches, four-wheeled oxcarts, and horse-drawn wagons crisscrossed Market Square. Farmers in long, loose smocks drove cows across from time to time, and tradesmen wheeled their wheelbarrows purposefully from one corner to another.

"Abraham Hanson" (a barber in Bangor, Maine) by Jeremiah Hardy. *Addison Gallery of Art, Phillips Academy, Andover, Massachusetts.*

Stately eighteenth-century mansions stood on the streets of Portsmouth, with massive chimneys, bright brass door knockers, and, high up under their roofs, garrets filled with old sea chests that held the odds and ends of two hundred years. China asters carpeted the front yards in summer, and out back the plum trees and gooseberry bushes crowded against the walls of the stables and carriage houses that opened onto the narrow lanes.

In winter's storms the giant elms dashed their branches against the gables of the stout old homes, and in the morning, banks of white barricaded people's front doors and sometimes reached halfway up their bedroom windows. Perhaps by noontime the plows, each drawn by four yokes of oxen, managed to break through the drifts. In the evening, when the temperature in the front halls of even the coziest houses had dropped toward zero, people pulled their chairs close to the fireplace and sipped warm cider while they played dominoes.

When the snow crust in the streets was thick enough to support men and horses, and when the icicles that hung from the eaves were a yard long, it was time to go coasting (and to repair smashed sleds), to skate on the frozen surface of the tidal river (and to trip headlong into eel holes in the ice). It was also time to build snow forts—for generations the boys of the North End and the boys of the South End had been feuding. They left snowballs out all night to freeze solid, some fortified with a small rock in the center. Each side counted its victories in terms of the other boys' black eyes and nosebleeds.

When spring came, coast youngsters grew restless. The scent of lilacs was always touched with the tang of salt. Children wandered on the beaches, gazing out to sea and listening to the crash and gurgle of the breakers. In the morning fogs they stumbled over kelp and driftwood and dead fish, and occasionally the swollen body of a drowned sailor or fisherman.

The dearest dream of a seaport boy was to own a row-boat or a small sailboat, probably in partnership with several of his friends, and be free to scramble down the slippery steps of the wharf and sneak off to explore the harbor.

Five Portsmouth twelve-year-olds set out on just such an excursion before sunrise one school day that had turned out to be an unexpected holiday when the master was called out of town. (They hardly ever had a free day otherwise for outings, for the Sabbath was out of the question.) They stowed away a bag of crackers, salt, sugar, half a dozen lemons, a piece of salt pork, pickles, and three gigantic apple pies, and they slung a keg of spring water over the side of the boat to keep it cold. They also took along crockery, some bricks, and a small tent. They rowed smoothly past misty banks that smelled of clover and at last landed on the river side of the farthest of the islands at the river mouth.

After they put up the tent in the pine woods, supporting it with oars, they went for a ramble and took a swim. On the seaward side they caught a nice batch of fish, including a cod. With the bricks they built a fireplace, skinned and cooked the fish, and ate them from clamshells. Late in the day they lay back to smoke "cigars" of sweet fern—and suddenly a squall blew up. The stranded boys huddled together in the gloom while the wind moaned and howled around them. At the height of the vicious storm their boat went adrift, with one of the boys in it!

A search party rescued the terrified boys the next morning. Several days later, the body of their friend was washed ashore on the point, near the graves of some early settlers who had been scalped by the Indians. Soon a small head-stone was put up to mark the new grave, behind a row of tall poplars at the water's edge. The boys never again went swimming from the point.

School took up most of children's time during most of the year. There was an academy for boys in Portsmouth, in a two-story brick building behind a picket fence, with small trees in the yard but no grass. The master's desk stood on a raised platform just inside the door, and in front of his desk was a recitation bench for fifteen or twenty pupils. There were several globes, and a blackboard the length of one wall. The boys sat at small green desks, placed far enough apart to keep them from whispering.

Every Wednesday morning each boy was required to lay a composition on the master's desk, written on a subject he had chosen the Monday before. Two prizes were awarded each month: the best composition earned the writer a pen-knife or a pencil case, and the worst entitled its author to wear a paper cap that proclaimed I AM A DUNCE.

After school the boys liked to return to the schoolyard to play ball and watch the girls from the Female Institute next door. As the girls filed out to shop for slate pencils and lemon drops they made eyes at the boys over the fence. The boys shoved notes into the hedge between the two school-yards for the girls to retrieve later.

Studying was impossible in the week before Indepen-dence Day. Boys ran about with their pockets bulging with Chinese firecrackers, while girls clung to each other and squealed. Though many people disapproved of the curious old custom, a certain group of town boys always built a bonfire on the square at midnight before the Fourth. They

"Entertainment of the Boston Rifle Rangers by the
Portland Rifle Club in Portland Harbor, August 12, 1829"
by Charles Codman. *The Brooklyn Museum.*

made a pyramid of barrels, set it ablaze, and joined hands
to dance around it, adding barrel staves to keep it going.

On the glorious day, villagers from miles around poured
into town. Twenty or thirty booths stood in a semicircle
around the square, gaily decorated with little flags and
loaded with cakes, gingerbread, lemonade, and root beer.
Fireworks, pinwheels, and punk were for sale at tables
nearby. The houses that bordered the square were decked
out in red, white, and blue bunting, and every street that
led to the center was arched over with evergreens entwined
with paper roses and patriotic mottoes. Church bells rang;

a brass band blared; and the air resounded with small-arms fire and the booming of old twelve-pounder cannon.

Portsmouth was full of useless black iron cannon from the War of 1812. At the corners of several streets that led away from the river there were many "old sogers," up-ended, with solid cannonballs soldered into their mouths. A dozen more of the rusty old twelve-pounders had been dumped in the grass on a deserted wharf at the foot of Anchor Lane. The wharf was covered with moss and weeds, and boys met there to fish and to play leapfrog on the backs of the abandoned guns.

The arrival, usually unexpected, of a great ship was a thrilling event in a sleepy, once busy seaport such as Portsmouth. One day a "man-o'-war" was sighted coming up the river. It anchored, and the boys of the town could hear the sailors singing as they lowered the longboat and scrambled over the side. Shopkeepers bustled about, delighted to have twenty or thirty tars in port all at one time. The two rival boardinghouse keepers, unused to such brisk business, hastily tidied up their run-down rooms. By midnight, the tipsy sailors, their battered tin dippers strapped around their waists, were roving through the otherwise silent streets of the town, shinnying up drainpipes, clutching at door knockers, and bellowing "Fire!"

Next day the ship sailed out of the harbor again. The shopkeepers sat down on their benches. Stray cats hunched down in the shadows of the waterfront, brooding over escaped rats and the kicks of sailors. The bluejays stopped scolding, and the pleasant old town settled down to its accustomed evening peace and quiet.

On Board a Merchantman

HUNDREDS of ambitious seaport boys went to sea at the age of twelve or thirteen, sometimes on their own fathers' ships. They went for the good pay, the travel, and the excitement, and bright, capable boys advanced rapidly. Most merchants felt that their customers would have more confidence in the "young men in the counting room" if the young men had been to sea, so they sent their sons on foreign voyages with family friends. Most boys started at the bottom and worked up.

There were two and sometimes more cabin boys on board each merchant ship, to wait on the officers, carry messages, and help the cook by taking the food from the galley to the seamen's quarters. They had a good chance to learn about sails, rigging, ship's time, and routine, perhaps taking the helm in fair weather and learning to use the navigational instruments. It was not unusual for a smart boy to rise through his own skill and daring to be a mate at twenty and a master at twenty-one.

Boys knew their places, however, and even though the captain might be a close friend back home, they referred to him as "the old man" behind his back, just as the rest of the crew did.

Foremast hands on Yankee ships, the "ordinary seamen" and the "able seamen," were the best paid, best fed, and most competent in the world. It was said of the Yankee sailor that every finger was a fishhook, to get hold of a loose, flapping sail and make it snug. He was known by his red-checkered shirt and blue bell-bottoms, topped by a blue pea jacket. On shore leave he dressed carefully in loose white duck trousers, white stockings, black pumps, clean shirt, black silk neckerchief (with a few dollars tied in the back of it), and well-varnished black hat, with a few feet of black ribbon streaming down over his eyes.

Most New England seamen knew how to read and write, and the vast majority of Yankee shipmasters "came in through the hawse hole"—the hole in the bow for the anchor cable—that is, they advanced from forecastle to cabin on their own merits. Shipmasters were considered gentlemen and were welcomed by local society in foreign ports. They were well educated and of good character, and were often part owners of the vessels they commanded. They had to know every detail of navigation and the handling of a ship. Every Yankee captain came to rely on the *Practical Navigator* by twenty-eight-year-old Captain Nathaniel Bowditch of Salem. Long adept at "dead reckoning" with compass, log, and sounding lead, New England seafarers navigated around the globe by taking lunar observations according to the brilliant young Bowditch's 1801 treatise (and it is still our standard guide to navigation). They also had to use excellent judgment in selling their cargoes and bringing home merchandise that would prove valuable at home.

One Salem captain, well known for his unusual degree of independence—sometimes too much for his employers' complete satisfaction—had sailed away on a pepper-buying voyage to Sumatra. On the way he heard by chance that the price of coffee in Arabia was reasonable, so he simply went to Mocha instead and took on a cargo of coffee. Back in Salem, the ship's owners secretly hoped that he *had* disobeyed orders this time, for the price of pepper had fallen and the price of coffee was high. For months they had no news of the ship, and they could hardly stand the suspense.

"The Sailor's Wedding" by Richard Caton Woodville.
The Walters Art Gallery.

When the ship came into port at last, the owners rowed
out to meet it, sniffing the air to leeward of the vessel.
Though it was considered extremely undignified to do so,
one of them hailed the captain.

"What's your cargo?"

"Pe-pe-pe-pep-per!" replied the captain, stifling a fake
sneeze.

But the air, to the delight of all, was distinctly scented with the aroma of fine coffee beans!

Yankee captains were famous the world over for being astonishingly young. They sent letters from ships to the owners in Salem or Boston with "P.S." messages asking the owners to "let Mother know I am well" and to do the same for the officers, who were perhaps all of eighteen years old. These young captains often left their commands to start their own merchant businesses at thirty, and by the time they reached the age of forty, were living in elegant retirement in fine houses.

The "supercargo" on board a merchant ship was a special representative of the owners and shippers and took no part in running the ship. He was likely to be a college graduate. He had to be intelligent, diplomatic, and good at supervising trade in foreign ports. (Sometimes a supercargo was promoted to command of a ship, and that was called "coming in through the cabin window.")

The first officer, or mate, was usually in line for a command of his own. The captain issued most of his orders through him. The mate supervised the men of each watch and was generally responsible for the performance and spirit of the crew. A good mate handled them strictly but fairly and won their respect. When a ship was getting under way, the captain observed the mate carefully—the mate, not the captain, was the busiest man on board that day.

Two or more lesser officers were quite a notch below the first mate, but like him they were always addressed as "Mr. ——." The "bo'sun," a sort of foreman who summoned the watches with the pipe he wore around his neck, was usually both smart and popular.

The cook (most likely a black man or a Chinese, for they

"The Navigator" by an unknown artist.
Abby Aldrich Rockefeller Folk Art Collection,
Williamsburg, Virginia.

were said to be the best) fixed the meals, and the steward
served the captain and officers. "Chips," the carpenter, and
"Sails," the sailmaker, were masters of their trades, neither
officers nor common seamen. The carpenter repaired "everything" in a small shop filled with lumber and wood
shavings. The sailmaker mended torn sails and made new
ones from the great rolls of canvas that all ships carried. He
sat on deck in fair weather, cross-legged, his hand protected

Two sailors aloft, engraving from a bank note.
The Metropolitan Museum of Art, Harris Brisbane Dick Fund, 1942.

by the leather palm. He held a large needle in his calloused fingers, and stuck spares into his broad leather bib. "Chips" and "Sails" worked whenever they were needed, which was often, and were generally good companions.

The common sailors lived in the forecastle, the dirty crowded triangle in the bow below decks. They never slept more than four hours at a time, after which the other watch went off duty and they were called. Each man had his own plate and spoon, but there was no table for their meals. One of the cabin boys brought the wooden "kid" or mess tub to the forecastle, and the men ate on the floor (or on deck), ladling their portions of grub onto their tin plates and cutting the tough slabs of salt beef with their pocket knives.

Whenever the steward opened a new barrel of salt beef, he picked over the meat and took out the best pieces—the ones with a little fat—for the cabin table. The seamen got the hardest, driest pieces, and they called the meat "old horse." There was a rumor that a Boston beef dealer had actually sold horsemeat as ship's stores. He was caught and sent to jail to stay until he had eaten it all himself. The story made the rounds on all the Yankee ships, and it was applauded by all!

Sunday—sometimes—meant a special treat, a plum duff made from flour-and-water dough sweetened with molasses and boiled up with raisins.

While the cabin's tea was brewed in a teapot and sweetened with real sugar, the crew's tea was made from loose tea leaves, water, and molasses boiled together. It was stirred before it was served so that each man got his fair share of leaves and sweetening. Every man got a quart night and morning, and drank it from a tin bucket.

Fresh drinking water was carried in an iron tank in the hold, and a scuttle butt filled with each day's supply of water stood on deck for the use of all. Far from land the men caught rainwater in buckets to add to the supply. When the supply ran low, one of the mates gave each man his daily ration of drinking water in the afternoon.

There was no fresh water available for washing, but in the torrential rainstorms in the tropics the men stopped up the scuppers (or deck drains) to trap the rainwater. They washed themselves and their clothes, splashing happily and using strips of canvas for towels. When the weather cleared, the ship's rigging was draped with clean shirts and pants, fluttering gaily as they dried in the burning hot sun.

Toward the middle of the nineteenth century, many captains took their families along with them on voyages, and since the cook and the steward took care of the meals and the seamen did the cleaning, the captains' wives had little housework. The children were expected to obey ship's rules just as everyone else did, for a ship was a cramped home and a dangerous one too.

The companionway to the captain's quarters was just forward of the wheel. The cabin had square windows up near the ceiling and a skylight as well, and across the hall there was usually a wooden toilet and possibly even a wooden tub for bathing. Tables and chairs were bolted to the floor, and there were few decorations on the walls. The captain and his family ate in the saloon with the mate, whether or not they really liked him personally.

The children had to stow their clothes and toys carefully, for no space was ever wasted on board ship. The youngsters were supposed to stay away from the forecastle and the galley. The sailors looked very interesting, but the children were not allowed to talk to them, nor to the cabin boy either even if they knew him well at home. Once in a while, after a visit in port, the sailors sent presents back to the children via the mate—coins or ribbons or whittled shark's teeth. Very rarely, if they were clean and neat and well shaven, the sailors were permitted to present their gifts in person.

"Chips," the carpenter, was the traditional friend and baby-sitter for the captain's children. The children were strictly forbidden to touch his tools, but it was Chips who took them for walks on deck in fair weather and escorted them ashore in foreign ports.

The sailors considered monkeys lucky and liked having them scurry about in the rigging, but seagoing children did not always find suitable pets. Cats did not like sailing ships, and large dogs, who missed a place to run, howled and whined and made the sailors nervous. Parrots used foul

Advertisement of a waterfront bookstore.
American Antiquarian Society.

language and were not considered proper pets for children. What pets there were in the captain's cabin were likely to be quite unusual—white cockatoos, Java squirrels, or small stray puppies from the islands of the South Pacific.

By the age of fourteen, children of sea captains were usually left at home to attend an academy or to enter college, but younger children led an exciting life at sea. Of course, they spent six mornings a week in the main cabin doing their lessons, using schoolbooks from home, with their mothers

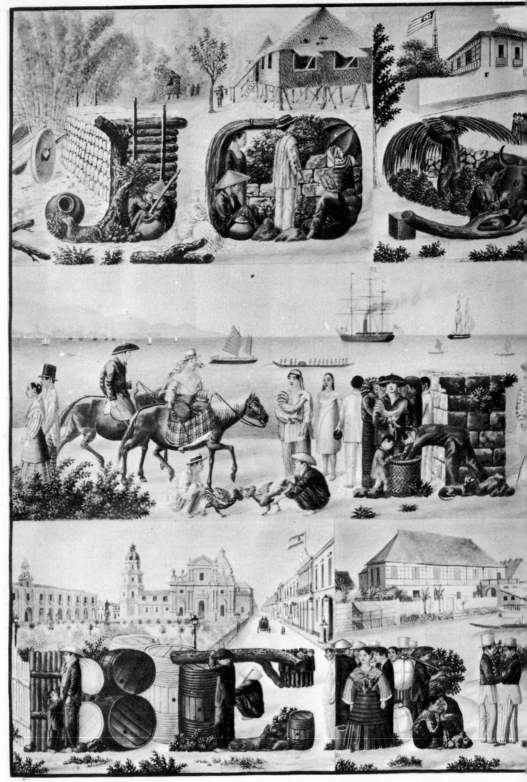

"Scenes in the Philippines," painted in Manila by José Honorato Lozato for Captain

Joseph Bertram of Salem. *Private collection.*

as teachers. Until the steward came in to set the table for noon dinner, they wrote compositions and read them aloud, drilled in spelling and multiplication, and studied their grammars and history books. But they learned their geography first-hand, and they found that arithmetic made sense when used in navigation. They observed the position of the stars and the moon and noted the changes in latitude and longitude and time as they sailed around the globe. "Chips" sometimes gave them drawing lessons, and they went on to more advanced subjects with the help of the young supercargo, fresh out of college.

Most sea captains' wives and children came to feel quite at home aboard ship. There was more spare time at sea than on land, and even the captains themselves were free to relax a little in fine weather. The captains worked on ship models, and their wives stitched elegant tucked shirts for their husbands to wear in port. The children played with rare seashells, coral, jade, and amber, and amused themselves for hours with Chinese puzzles and menageries of carved ivory animals.

After visiting a dozen foreign ports, Yankee families even began to feel a little out of place at home in New England. Hundreds of Yankee children circled the globe on sailing ships before they set foot in towns twenty miles from home, for land travel was more difficult in those days. Seaport children looked to the sea, and their horizons were broad indeed.

Outward Bound Around the World

Bᴇᴛᴡᴇᴇɴ the Revolution and the War of 1812, the great wealth of Salem came mainly from the China trade. Later, Boston and New York took the lead in trading with the Orient.

Each year, as the Chinese ships, laden with teas, came down the Pearl River from the interior of their country, the foreign merchant vessels sailed up the river with the south-west monsoon wind to the anchorage at Whampoa. The *hoppo*, or Chinese customs collector, boarded each foreign ship to measure it for *cumshaw* ("grateful thanks") duty, taxing every ship and accepting gifts for himself and his relatives and encouraging handsome bribes. Then the cargo

"Canton Factories, 1804" by a Chinese artist.
Courtesy of the Peabody Museum of Salem.

was taken twelve miles upstream to Canton and landed at the *hongs* that the traders leased from the Chinese.

The Canton *hongs*, or factories, faced the river, on a thousand-foot frontage of swampy land. No goods were manufactured there—these factories were trade centers that contained showrooms, warehouses, vaults, and luxurious bachelor living quarters for the foreign merchants' agents. (No women were ever allowed in Canton, so the resident agents' wives and families lived all year in the nearby Portuguese colony of Macao, and the traders joined them in the spring after the business season was over.)

The buildings ran back about a quarter of a mile to Old China Street, where the exporters had their shops, and several lanes cut through the factories. Runners from Hog Lane led eager sailors back to the curio shops and grog shops of the quarter, where the young Yankees were fed pork chops and boiled eggs and tea—and plenty of rum to help open up their pockets.

Great junks glided down the river, junks with eyes painted on their bows, lacquered topsides, festoons of flags, and square sails of brown matting. The stately mandarin boats had two banks of oars, and the little sampans, or houseboats, formed a permanent floating city. The boats of provisions dealers and toy vendors and the skiffs of barbers bobbed about, and canal boats and ferries plied their routes across the river. At twilight the atmosphere was magical; the boats, moored on bamboo poles stuck in the mud bottom near the shore, rocked gently in the soft pastel light of paper lanterns.

Since "foreign devils" were allowed only on one short section of the Canton waterfront, all foreign trade was handled through a dozen very rich merchant princes ap-

Blue and white jar from China.
The Metropolitan Museum of Art.
Bequest of Benjamin Altman, 1913.

pointed by the emperor to take care of every monotonous detail. There were no banks or written contracts, but luckily these men were the most honorable in the world.

The high-born Chinese merchants, resplendent in their silks and brocades, got along well with the Yankees; in fact, they liked them much better than the rather arrogant British traders. The Yankees worked hard at learning Chinese and were generous and polite to the princes. While the English sailed up in their lumbering fifteen-hundred-ton East Indiamen, owned by rich chartering companies, the young Yankee captains arrived in small, fast, individually owned ships manned by teen-age crews. Yankee officers were at home all over the world, tactful but competitive, and they soon took much of the China trade away from the old, established British East India Company.

The Yankees all took advantage of a privilege called the "private adventure," the chance to make a little profit or special purchase on the side. One sixteen-year-old cabin boy took a walk around the sailors' city and Hog Lane but prudently spent his shore leave investing his small savings in some silk handkerchiefs to sell back home in Boston. Most

Yankee seafarers left home with requests and orders from friends and relatives, including children, for silks, shawls, jewelry, and candied ginger.

In the spring, when the Yankee ships were loaded and ready to catch the northeast monsoon down to the China Sea, the captains worried most about getting the cargo safely home to Boston or Salem, undamaged by cockroaches. The roaches ate labels off tea chests, devoured sailors' oiled clothing and boots, and even nibbled the men's toenails as they slept. Sailors swore that unless they slept with their boots in their bunks, they would find nothing in the morning but metal eyelets and nails. So, before sailing time, Chinese came aboard with baited baskets, and easily caught thirty bushels of cockroaches in a single day. The vessels were smoked with charcoal and sulphur fumes to drive out the rats, and then it was homeward bound.

There were hundreds of miles of dangerous islands and reefs and shoals to navigate, through waters infested by savage Malay pirates, until the welcome sight of Java Head rose up, its terraced peaks crowned with palm groves and rice paddies. The air was heavy with the scent of flowers as the trading ships stopped for fresh provisions before continuing on their course. The Boston merchant ships then proceeded westward around the world past the Cape of Good Hope, while the Salem ships continued home around Cape Horn according to custom, for Salem captains preferred to round the globe in an easterly direction.

One typical cargo from China, landed at Boston in 1810, brought its merchant-owners a profit of more than two hundred thousand dollars. There were fifty sets of blue and white dinnerware, nearly five hundred tea sets, nine hundred chests of tea, two hundred chests of cinnamon-like

cassia, thousands of pieces and bales of sturdy blue, white, and yellow "nankeen" cloth, ninety cases of silks (black, blue-and-white striped, and brown), and some "gentlemen's satins" in stripes of bottle green and black.

For marvelous goods such as these the Americans had at first little to offer the Chinese. The English could afford to pay in silver for their teas and silks, but the Yankees had to find something else of value to trade. They soon became specialists in delivering costly luxury articles for the mandarins' tables and wardrobes.

The Chinese princes adored the rich and lustrous fur of the sea otter for robes, capes, and trimmings. They could not get enough from Russia, and clamored particularly for the large pelts that reached from a man's chin to his toes, the thick, soft furs of choicest black-brown. Smart Yankees from Boston promptly entered the fur business, off the northwest coast of North America, and made tremendous profits. Soon the Indians of the coast were calling *any* American a "Boston man."

The *Columbia*, the first American vessel to circle the globe, made the pioneering voyage of nearly forty-two thousand miles in 1787–1790, and before long, Boston ships and brigs were leaving each fall to round the Horn in the Antarctic summer and be on "the Coast" by spring, around Nootka Sound, Vancouver Island. The usual northwest voyage lasted about three years. Quite a few twelve or fourteen-year-old New England lads first went to sea on "Nor'west-men." A voyage to the Northwest Coast or to Russian America (Alaska), returning around the world by way of China and the Pacific Islands, outranked all other voyages in mystery, adventure, glamour—and profit.

On the rainy coast the Nor'westmen, heavily armed to ward off attacks by hostile Indians, anchored in one rocky cove after another to obtain sea-otter pelts from the natives by barter. The Indians ran along the shore and quickly sailed out to the ships in canoes filled with furs and salmon. They swapped a salmon for a nail, and for a pocket mirror, they turned over a nearly black, glossy sea-otter skin that would bring $50, $80, even $120 in Canton. They resented the intruders, but they longed for the goods and trinkets the

Yankees brought—mirrors, cloth, rings, shoes, beads, trousers, and jackets. Iron collars and bracelets became such a rage among the Indians along the coast that some vessels took along metal workers to make ornaments to order.

The regular pay on the Northwest fur-trade route to Canton was higher than that on any other trade route. Besides, the masters and mates got a percentage of the proceeds and also had a "privilege," space allotted for several tons of private purchases they could take home and sell. With fair luck a young captain on a Northwest and China voyage could return with a personal profit of twenty-five hundred dollars, a very large sum of money in those days.

Sealskins, although not as valuable as sea-otter pelts, were still a fair substitute to trade in Canton for tea, silks, jade, and teakwood, so ambitious Yankees lost little time in tracking down these animals as well. American sealers first visited the Juan Fernández Islands, in the Pacific Ocean off Chile, in 1797. Vessels "bound 'round the Horn a-skinning" stopped off at the treeless Falkland Islands in the South Atlantic for fresh water and green vegetables, excellent peat for fuel, and the eggs of small penguins and other sea birds. The New Englanders kept half-wild herds of cattle, hogs, and sheep on the Falklands to supply themselves with meat. The men exchanged news with special enthusiasm, for most of them came from the little port of Stonington, Connecticut.

Sealing vessels, though quite small, had to be stout enough to weather the terrific gales of the Antarctic passage. Inside the hulls the walls dripped constantly because of the icy sea that surrounded them. The vessels also had to be easily maneuverable; for when the sealers spotted a well-camouflaged brownish-black seal herd on a rocky shore, they rode right onto the beach in pursuit.

Then men stunned the slow, clumsy animals with hickory clubs, skinned them, and washed the pelts at the water's edge, tossing scraps of blubber to fish so hungry that they too could be clubbed from shore. The seals were so plentiful and so easy to capture that the vessels were soon ready to sail home with hundreds of thousands of salted-down skins to be stretched and dried for the markets of China. Sometimes even the captain's cabin and the crew's quarters were partially crammed with stacks of skins.

For quick profits that could amount to three times the cost of the vessel and all its gear, the sealers trapped the animals so heedlessly that within ten years the 3,500,000 seals of the Juan Fernández Islands were nearly wiped out.

Then, around 1820, the rich rookeries of the South Shetland Islands were discovered, where the South Atlantic meets the South Pacific. It took just two years for the Yankee sealers to destroy these herds too. Young "bachelor" seals could be taken without endangering the life of the herds, but the sealers failed to spare the bulls who headed families of twenty-five or thirty females with their cubs. So the seals were doomed.

The sealers, tough and bold, were great explorers who went to the ends of the earth in uncharted oceans and returned home with tales of eerie islands sighted in the midst of gales, then lost forever. They tended to keep quiet about where they found their prey, and their logbooks were purposely vague. Their favorite secret meeting place was Deception Island, where the cold air merged with warm, steaming water in silent, swirling fog. The hidden bay, five miles across, filled the circular cone of a submerged volcano. Other mariners who knew nothing of the island's existence could sail by and never realize it was there at all.

This mysterious place was discovered by twenty-one-year-old Captain Nathaniel Palmer of Stonington, who was said to possess a kind of telescopic vision that allowed him to see things few other men could. In his homemade cap and his sealskin boots, standing on the deck of his thirty-eight-foot sloop, young Nat Palmer became the first human being to sight the vast continent of Antarctica, at the great white peninsula that now bears his name, 650 miles south of wild Cape Horn.

During the same years, the seafarers of Salem were navigating the tricky waters of the Malay Archipelago without published charts. Salem ships had pioneered the Sumatra pepper trade for profits of 700 per cent! The War of 1812, which disrupted foreign trade for several years, ruined much of Salem's old prosperity. While fast-growing Boston absorbed the foreign trade of every other New England port, Salem ships carried on a mixed-cargo trade in exotic specialties. They left with goods from New England, the South, and the West Indies—butter, lard, beef, codfish, chocolate, rum, brandy, ale, candles, soap, flints, whale oil, iron, pottery, chairs, tobacco—and sometimes stopped at Madeira to pick up choice wines. Then they sailed on to India, where they sold the American goods and the wines, and took on cotton cloth, spices, and sugar.

These Salem vessels called at one South Sea island after another as they carried on a trade in tortoiseshell, pearls, mother-of-pearl shell, and fragrant sandalwood—all greatly desired in Canton.

Sandalwood was considered to be the property of royalty in the isles of the Pacific. Salem captains discovered it growing wild in the Sandwich Islands (Hawaii). The Chinese wanted the wood to make furniture, boxes, fans, and oil to

"King Kamehameha I of Hawaii" by an unknown artist.
The Boston Athenæum.

scent gilt-edged incense paper. The Yankees and the
Hawaiian chieftains cut the wood so fast that within a few
years it was all gone. By that time, in fact, there was so
much sandalwood in Canton that the price fell, and the
greediest of the traders made no profits at all.

Salem merchantmen also dealt in fancy food specialties
beloved by the wealthy Chinese. Only the very richest Chinese could afford to dine on bird's-nest soup. The nests used
in the soup were built by swifts in clefts on rocky coasts.
Two men gathered them from a boat, one hooking the nests
with a long pole and the other catching them in a scoop net.
They cleaned away the feathers and dirt and dried the

nests in the sun, for they turned moldy and soft when wet. The nests were packed carefully for shipment in boxes lined with thick paper mats.

The oddest Salem specialty was *bêche-de-mer*, slimy sea slugs for the soup tureens of the mandarins. The slugs (also known as sea cucumbers) lived in huge numbers in the shallows and coral reefs of the Fiji Islands, where the islanders were fierce and unpredictable. The *bêche* trade was a dangerous business in which men risked their lives for fantastic profits.

Native fishermen were hired to gather the slugs by torchlight or moonlight, while other gangs of natives erected long, thatched drying sheds on the beach. The slugs were drained, slit, cleaned, and boiled in black iron pots. Fiji cannibals may have used these same pots to boil people, but they preferred roasting them.) Day and night the workers skimmed and ladled and laid out the slugs on racks in the sheds for curing. Young seamen supervised as the islanders tended the slow-burning fires, for the sheds kept catching fire and new sections had to be built to replace the charred parts. When the job was done, the natives were paid off with guns, knives, scissors, hatchets, fishhooks, cloth, mirrors, blue beads, and whale teeth.

Salem ships traded in gum copal for varnish at Zanzibar and Madagascar. Small brigs and schooners called at fever-infested ports in West Africa, bringing clocks, cottons, pots and pans, foodstuffs, furniture, and shoes from New England, and returning with gold dust, ivory, palm oil, and peanuts. And in the 1830s, Salem vessels began bringing back Pará rubber overshoes from Brazil. The rubbers stiffened in cold weather and melted in the summer, but they were just the thing for New England's slushy streets. They were so useful, in fact, that Salem ships imported 750,000 pairs in seven years' time.

Boston ships had traded with the West Indies long before the Revolution, and Boston merchants still stuck to the custom of "trying all ports," trading wherever possible, in whatever possible. After the Northwest fur trade declined, Boston owner-merchants continued to send cargoes "up the Straits" (past Gibraltar) to Mediterranean ports: sugar, coffee, beeswax, lumber, tobacco, "domestics" (cotton textiles of New England manufacture), cheese, rum, soap, shoes, barrels, hams, codfish, and pickled salmon from the rivers of Maine. They carried East India goods and Havana cigars to Europe and returned with lemons, oranges, salt, feathers, wines, raisins, currants, nuts, wool, cork, and olive oil. They even carried blocks of ice from Maine and Massachusetts rivers and ponds, packed in pine sawdust, to Kingston and Havana and Rio, Calcutta, Manila, and Canton! Boston vessels outran the pirates of the Levant to swap clocks, cottons, rum, and candles for drums of dried figs from Smyrna, and for wool and carpets that had been brought by triangular-sailed feluccas and camel trains to the bazaars of Araby.

Boston merchant ships brought home sperm oil and whale oil that had been left off in the Azores by outward-bound whalers for shipment to New England. Ships loaded with tea and rum detoured southward to pick up Georgia cotton and Cuban sugar, and they used the tea and rum and cotton and sugar to pay for canvas, linens, furs, hemp, and iron in Russian and Swedish ports. The harpoon makers of New Bedford preferred Russian iron, but the shipsmiths of Plymouth wanted the Swedish kind.

Fast, capacious brigs called "fruiters" hurried to reach

Boston by Thanksgiving with their cargoes of grapes and oranges. They came in from Rio and the West Indies with their booms and spars hung with bunches of bananas reserved for their owners and special friends.

From South America, where the people were eager for the China silks and Indian shawls the Yankee vessels brought, Boston ships obtained great quantities of sheepskin, tallow,

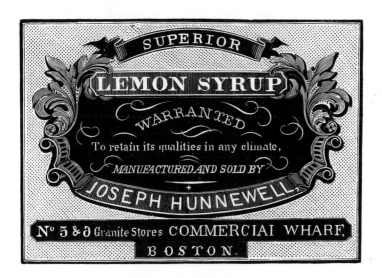

and hides. Beautiful Rio, with its twinkling lights and lovely girls, was a favorite port of call for Yankee sailors. From there, it was on around the Horn for Pacific island trading, with a stop in Honolulu to deliver blankets and ticking, cottons, shoes, umbrellas, and groceries for the resident Yankees and to take on whalebone and oil left by the whalers.

As New England turned more and more to manufacturing, ships rounded the Horn for the coast of Mexican California to get hides to supply the shoemaking shops of Massa-

Mission of St. Louis (the Bishop) about the middle of the old territory. S. luis Obispo.

Dec. 27.
NCal.

"San Luis Obispo Mission, 1848" by William Rich Hutton.
The Huntington Library, San Marino, California.

chusetts. At anchor three miles offshore in the long swells of the Pacific, sailors listened to the roll of the surf and the silver sound of mission bells. Yankees and Kanakas (Polynesian seamen) collected, cured, and stored the hides they called "California bank notes," to be sold in Boston for twice their cost.

Sunny California was a curious place, at once bleak and beautiful—lazy, dusty, and very different from New England. Dogs and pigs ran wild, the descendants of animals put ashore by numberless vessels that had called on the dreamy coast. One time several young sailors on liberty hired horses and rode out to an old Spanish mission where they asked politely if they might buy a meal. The gracious friars invited them inside. Indian boys served them baked meats, beans with onions and peppers, boiled eggs, noodles, and wine—the best meal the seamen had eaten in many months—but the gentle friars would accept no payment.

Ships spent months, even years, beating up and down the coast until the holds were full of hides. Only then, at last, was it time to leave for Boston. "Time for us to go!" rang the chorus. Up came the anchor; cheers and salutes echoed from other vessels across the bay. In a light breeze the ship was under way. Casks were full of sweet fresh water. The longboat was filled to the gunwales with fragrant hay, for there were a dozen sheep huddled in the forward pen. Under the bow of the longboat, an equal number of pigs squealed excitedly.

Weeks later, the ship was only inching forward, more in the water than on it. All sails were furled, and the lee rail was buried in the mountainous seas off Cape Horn. Suddenly a great wave poured over the ship. In an instant the sheep pen, the pigsty, and the galley disappeared. The captain's cabin was swamped, and the mate was washed out of his bunk below. But the ship shook free, and the cook managed to crawl out from under the galley shed that lay bottoms-up among the broken boards of the sheep pen. The sailors set the sodden sheep and the furious pigs on their feet again and put them in the longboat.

At sea, disasters that ended well were immediately turned into jokes, so after the sailors had set up the galley again, they roared with laughter at the sight of the tough salt beef for the forecastle lying high and dry like a rock upon the deck, while the soggy remains of the fine chicken pie and pancakes for the cabin lay drowned in a salty puddle.

A ship, unlike a person, "puts on its best suit in bad weather," so the sailors set new sails to run the Horn, saving the old ones to put back later. Green walls of water slammed repeatedly into the nearly vertical deck, and the sails slatted and boomed like cannon on the Fourth of July. (It was winter in the Southern Hemisphere, but it was, in fact, Independence Day in Boston, where the girls were at that moment strolling with their parasols up and daintily eating sweet ices in the sunshine!)

An old sow was on board who had already been twice around the Cape of Good Hope and once before around Cape Horn. One miserable night the sailors heard her groaning and found her nearly frozen to death on deck in snow and hail. They wrapped her up in an old sail and bedded her down in straw, and she did not move until fair weather.

Just off the Horn the sun broke through, and the sailors gazed in horror at an iceberg several hundred feet high, its center dark blue, its base encrusted with frozen foam, its top crowned with snow. Thunder seemed to shake the ship as chunks of ice broke off and fell, in weird slow motion, into the water.

The vessel rounded the Horn safely, and one day the weather seemed a little milder. The men swept the snow off the deck and strewed the deck with ashes to make it less slippery. And then it rained and rained. At sea nothing, not even a snowstorm, is worse than the cold rain that wets a poor sailor's clothing through and through.

Weeks passed, and then one day the ship entered the warm current of the Gulf Stream. Clouds filled the sky. The wind blew hard from the northeast against the current and churned up a sea so ugly and choppy that even a lad who

"On Board the *Peruvian*, 1831" by "H.S."
Courtesy of the New-York Historical Society, New York City.

had been at sea two years could not go aloft without becoming seasick.

More weeks passed. The ship was approaching the New England coast. The variations of the ocean bottom were so dependable that the mate did not even have to look for land to know exactly where they were. He simply took soundings—black mud off Block Island, dark sand toward Nantucket, then sand and white shells, then white sand alone. The men cleaned out their sea chests and laid out their going-ashore clothes, and they threw their worn caps and mittens overboard.

As the low sand hills of Cape Cod came into view, the ship began firing its guns for a pilot. The waters were alive with sails—square-riggers outward bound, coasters, schooners—steamers too. The men ran the signals up the foremast, and within half an hour, the owner in his counting room would know his ship was safely in. And the boardinghouse keepers of the waterfront would know that a ship was in from 'round the Horn with a crew paid off with two years' wages all at once!

For many months the men had dreamed of home, yet most of them felt strangely let down at the sight of the town. All hands cleared the decks, loaded the guns for the salute, and loosed the sails. Up the harbor they went! With a chorus that woke half the folk of the North End they hauled the ship into the wharf and made her fast.

The decks soon swarmed with customhouse officers, news agents, and boardinghouse runners who smilingly pretended to recognize the young sailors personally and gave them their cards and offered to cart their things up to town.

The crew furled the sails and were dismissed. Boys two years before, they had grown into strong young men, hair long and faces bronzed by the tropic sun. As they straggled slowly ashore in twos and threes to roam the streets of the port, they saw one of the mates disappearing around a corner. He was pulling a handcart that contained his worn sea chest, his mattress, and his precious box of navigational instruments. They envied him, for he was hurrying home to enjoy a home-cooked meal and a whole night's sleep in his own bed.

II
Fishing
on the North Atlantic

Come all ye young sailormen, listen to me,
I'll sing you a song of the fish in the sea.
Then blow ye winds westerly, westerly blow,
We're bound to the south'ard, so steady she goes!

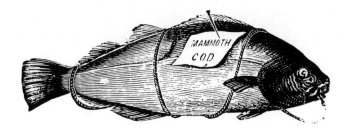

"Fishermen at Sea," attributed to James Hamilton.
Courtesy, Webb Gallery of American Art,
Shelburne Museum, Shelburne, Vermont.

Cape Cod and Cape Ann

WHEN THE EARLY SETTLERS arrived in Massachusetts, they found a double treasure: timber and fish. With the timber they built ships to go out after the fish that filled the bays and offshore waters. The plentiful cod became the basis for a profitable trade with the West Indies.

The Grand Banks fisheries, on the sandy shallows off the Newfoundland coast, were well established quite early. Cape Ann "Bankers" made two or three trips a year. Some small vessels dried the white fish on the shores of Nova Scotia, while others salted their catch just enough to bring it back and then finished curing the fish on the sands and ledges of beaches near home port. The New England shores were lined for miles with "fish flakes," drying racks of woven branches on posts, some thirty inches off the ground.

The cod was graded into three types. The lowest grade, called "Jamaica fish," was traded in the West Indies for molasses and sugar. The middle grade was saved for home consumption—the salt cod that Thoreau said looked like "yellow birch with the bark left on." The largest and best cod were split, salted, and kept on the flakes for several weeks before being piled up in the dark, covered with salt hay. The fish were uncovered, restacked, and pressed down, and with luck, after two or three months, they were ripe and dun-colored by late summer. This "dunfish" was a great delicacy, and much of it was exported to the Catholic countries of Europe for Friday and holy-day meals.

The town of Marblehead, near Salem, was a leading fishing port, although its harbor was open to wild storms from the northeast. The land around Marblehead was hilly and strewn with boulders. The people had the reputation, in other towns, of being somewhat peculiar. Marblehead urchins delighted in hurling stones at "furriners" from Salem or Lynn or Boston. The town never grew really wealthy, but its schooners were eventually the largest and best in all New England.

Gloucester, first a trading village, grew into an important fishing port that gradually absorbed the rest of the Cape Ann fisheries, but the old village was always known as "the Harbor." In storms, some forty or fifty vessels would tie up at Gloucester. A few men always stayed to take care of the boats, while the rest of the skippers and crews walked to their homes in the village or over in Sandy Bay (now known as Rockport). The cheerful three-story houses of Gloucester were rather plain, but they were furnished with very personal treasures and mementoes.

All of Cape Cod had only one real harbor, at Provincetown; but Provincetown, out at the tip of the cape, was too isolated to become a trading center. The lanes of the place were covered with light sand as soft as drifting snow, and fish flakes lined each side of them instead of shrubs and

Fish weathervane. *National Gallery of Art, Index of American Design.*

"Appleton's Wharf, Marblehead" by an unknown artist.
Courtesy of the Peabody Museum of Salem.

flowers. The village, in fact, was one long street with a chain of sand hills right behind the houses, and every alley led to the beaches.

Provincetown had the largest fishing fleet on the Cape, but every other creek or tidal inlet had its fishing fleet as well. The Cape had no water power, so there were never many factories, and the railroad passed it by. But there were towns where every boy and man between twelve and forty-five went to sea for his living. The sea was so much a part of life that one Provincetown boy, who stared hard at a traveler's wagon, wondered out loud how the thing could go so straight without a rudder.

Boys and men who did not go to sea made ships and gear for those who did, and small boys and old men worked the farms on Cape Cod. Boat fishermen supplied fresh fish in winter, and other fisherfolk farmed the oyster beds and clam flats, shucking and barreling clams for use as codfish bait.

Early in the Revolutionary War the British had cut off the supply of salt that was essential in preserving fish and meat in the days before refrigeration was invented, so a new industry grew up on Cape Cod: extracting salt from seawater. By the 1830s more than 650 saltworks were turning out half a million bushels of salt per year. The main "street" of Provincetown was the beach, lined with rows and rows of windmills that pumped seawater into pine vats for evaporation. The vats were shallow, with covers to keep rainwater out, and the bright sun produced great quantities of salt by drying up the water without the use of fuel.

Windmills were very important on Cape Cod and the

"Provincetown" by John Warner Barber.
Society for the Preservation of New England Antiquities.

Masthead of a Cape Cod newspaper.

offshore islands, where there were no rushing streams to provide the power to grind grain. It was hard to find a man who had the skill to build a proper windmill. In Colonial days, millwrights and millers had been exempt from military service because they were so important to the people of the villages. It was not an easy job to run the seacoast mills built of heavy oak timbers and rigged with strips of canvas for sails. Many of the millers were strong and weather-beaten former sailors retired from the sea.

The windmills were set back from the highroads because they frightened horses. Cape Cod boys used to risk their necks riding on windmills, weaving themselves between the slats of a mill arm and whirling around fifty feet off the ground. The trick was to jump off at precisely the right moment, and a very tricky trick it was.

Ship's carpenters built tight against wind and weather the snug cottages in which the Cape Codders lived. The walls of the houses bulged slightly outward from floor to roof, like the hulls of ships. The roofs were crusty with moss, as rusty-looking as old anchors.

Cape Cod folk were thrifty, and few were very, very poor. One mother, a shipmaster's wife, made all her own clothes and the clothes for her five children. She bought raw wool and cotton in Boston and spent all winter spinning at home. Then, when summer came, she and her children spent at

least an hour weaving every morning, before they went out
to feed the animals and make breakfast. That way each
child could have a new woolen suit and two new striped or
checkered cotton suits or dresses each year.

Cape Cod folk ate well—much better than the farmers
inland. They liked a hearty breakfast of brown bread and
butter, salt or fresh fish, pie sometimes, and tea or coffee.
For midday dinner, they ate dishes such as boiled salt meat,
fresh fish, salt fish with salt pork, baked beans, wild fowl,
Indian pudding, and root vegetables. "Cape Cod turkey"
was salt cod or haddock simmered until tender and served
with a thin gravy of milk, flour, and salt pork.

Boys and girls picked up plenty of lobsters on the shore at
low tide. June meant a treat of fresh peas (and pea pods to
sail in the tide pools). And in September beach plums grew
juicy and tangy, for jelly. The cranberry grew wild in the
marshes and even in sand, wherever underground water fed
the bushes, and turned from ivory to ruby in the crisp chill
of late October.

Family-manned vessels were not at all unusual on Cape
Cod. Many young men first went to sea on coasters or fishing boats, and then shipped out from Boston and New York
to sail the seven seas. The little town of Brewster, with no
harbor of its own, was famous as the birthplace of sea captains—it boasted more native masters and mates than any
other town its size in the United States, and once numbered
ninety-nine living sea captains among its citizens! One such
captain first went to sea as cook and cabin boy on a voyage
from Boston to Surinam at a wage of $3.50 a month. He
made the trip from his home to Boston on a packet schooner,
and paid for his ticket with two bushels of homegrown corn.
When he returned from the West Indies voyage, he had

"View of Gloucester Harbor" by Fitz Hugh Lane. *Virginia Museum.*

saved twenty dollars in silver to present to his widowed
mother.

Fishermen's sons swarmed all over their fathers' vessels as
soon as they could walk. Soon they were fishing with hand-
lines off the rock ledges and begging to be taught to row.
Their sisters hung back enviously, already knowing that
they would spend many hours on the beach year after year,
waiting anxiously for their boys and men to return safely.

Little boys had good reason to help their mothers around
the house. Boys ten or twelve years old did the cooking on
the Gloucester and Marblehead fishing boats in the years
following the Revolution, and the tradition lasted even
longer on Cape Cod. After a couple of trips as cook, the
boys handed down their iron pots and long spoons to their
little brothers or cousins and began their fisherman's apprenticeship. They learned to lure the cod, and to head,

split, and salt down the fish. Every boy's grandest ambition was to save enough money to buy a schooner of his own and live on shore on the vessel's earnings. It cost less to buy and equip a fishing vessel than a merchant ship or a whaleship, and the earnings were likely to be fairly steady.

Some fishing vessels were owned by groups of men who furnished all supplies and sold the catch wholesale. Each fisherman received half the value of his catch, and the skipper got a bonus besides. On Cape Cod, particularly, fishing vessels were usually owned in one-sixteenth shares, sometimes partly by their own crews and partly by retired sea captains, widows, or orphans. The owners usually furnished basic essentials such as salt meat, biscuits, and ship's supplies, and took back the cost before paying the crew at the end of the voyage. The owners got a quarter to a third of the profits, and the rest was divided among the crew in proportion to each man's share of the catch.

Every fisherman furnished his own lines and gear. A fisherman's full rig consisted of a tarred canvas hat, a jacket of sheepskin or goatskin, a stout leather apron, baggy calfskin pants, and huge broad boots of cowhide with tops that could be turned up high over the knees. (It was some years before oilskins and "sou'westers" came into general use.)

His rig was heavy and cumbersome, but it protected him well against the wet and the cold.

New England fishermen seldom left the fisheries for the merchant fleet in spite of the prestige that ships' officers enjoyed. They preferred their own traditional way of life— the short voyages, the relaxed discipline on board, and the chance to be at home much of the time. They shared in the profits of each trip, and though many of them ended the idle season in debt for groceries, they liked being "on their own hook."

The typical vessel of the Cape Ann coves was the "Chebacco," built by the fishermen themselves and owned on shares. Chebacco was the old Indian name for the town of Essex, where the boats were built. Chebaccos were double-ended, with sharp, or "pink," ends, and rigged with main and foresails. Easy to handle, they rode the waves like ducks

"Ship-building, Gloucester Harbor" by Winslow Homer.
Courtesy of the Fogg Art Museum, Harvard University, Gift of W. G. Russell Allen.

and were considered seaworthy enough to sail all the way to Labrador. Mostly, they went out after cod and haddock along the coast of Maine or within a hundred miles of Eastern Point near Gloucester. Chebacco fishermen moored their boats on half-submerged dead-tree roots and went home to tiny cottages in windswept coves. Every village, though, had its favorite type of boat—the Sandy Bay boys their small, flat-bottomed wherries, the Cape Codders their round-bottomed whaleboats.

Eventually, "pinkies," light schooners that were really improved Chebaccos, were used in the cod and mackerel fisheries. They were dry and comfortable in choppy waters and had no rails or bulwarks above the deck amidships. In the small forward apartment, or "cuddy," were two berths and a brick fireplace with a wood chimney plastered inside for protection against fire.

"Jiggers," developed in the 1830s, appeared to be chunky, clumsy, square-sterned, and barrel-sided, but they were quite capable of sailing anywhere in the world. Gaily painted in yellow, green, black, and white, they mounted easily to the crests of the waves and settled in the hollows on an almost even keel. All the cooking on a jigger, including brewing tea and coffee, was still done in a large iron pot over a brick hearth. The chimney came out flush with the deck, and on top of it was a box or funnel that could be removed. All the time the smoke flowed freely up—or down! Whenever a fine fish was hooked, the crew hung the best cuts from the cabin beams, and by the end of the voyage the pieces of fish were deliciously cured by the smoke. The fish was divided among the men of the crew, and smoked halibut fins and napes were considered extra special presents on the coast of old Massachusetts.

There were few wharves in Gloucester. Fishing vessels were moored in the harbor on oak stumps that had been sunk into the bottom. Fitted over the stumps, logs rode easily up and down with the tide. Each log held a floating piece of cable with a loop at the end, ready to be slipped over the bow of a pinkie to make it fast.

The Gloucester haddock fleet began getting ready about April first. The men ran the boats onto the beach and had them caulked and coated with pitch on the bottom. Then the sails were fastened, and the stores taken aboard: molasses, fat salt pork, flour, hard crackers, water, and a little rum—simple fare to last about a week. A box of tinder and some homemade matches were absolutely essential, though struggling with foul-smelling brimstone matches and tinder was sure to make any boy "heave up" in rough seas! The fishermen spent two to seven days out and marketed their catch at Charlestown, from where hawkers took the fish to Boston in handcarts and sold them at retail.

About 1830, Gloucester fishermen (and Cape Codders soon after) first went out to Georges Bank, a hundred miles east of the Cape, where the sucking currents, shoals, and sudden squalls had long frightened fishermen away. One old fisherman recalled his first trip to Georges after halibut—they ate fish three quarters of the time, along with hard bread and salt meat. Hard bread fried in pork fat was the standard meal, but the favorite was "Dundee pudding," which was just hard bread pounded up and sweetened with molasses, with a little flour mixed in to stick it all together.

Halibut was so plentiful then that often the vessels did not even have to anchor. Two schooners once brought in full "fares" from Georges after only seventy-two hours away from port. "Smacks," vessels that carried no ice but had

wet wells amidships with holes to let the salt water in, brought fish to Boston alive, where they were unloaded, cleaned, iced, and shipped inland by railroad.

The mackerel boats, steadied with a load of pebbles for ballast, carried hogsheads on deck, each with a hole and a plug. These tubs were filled with salt water, and the dressed fish were put in. The water was drained and changed every hour, and the fishermen aimed to get the mackerel to Boston

"Ships in Ice off Ten
Pound Island, Gloucester"
by Fitz Hugh Lane.
*M. & M. Karolik Collection.
Courtesy, Museum of
Fine Arts, Boston.*

before daylight and sell them in the cool of the early morning. There were three men and two boys to a boat. They fished through the season, sharing equally, and considered fifty dollars a week quite a good take.

Mackerel were elusive fish—at times abundant and then suddenly nowhere to be found. Boys could easily help with the "jigging," using small lines and a simple hook with a lead or pewter plummet cast around its shank. As the vessel

89

drifted slowly, the men threw the bait overboard to attract the fish. In the early days they ground up herring or other small fish under the heels of their boots for bait, or chopped bait during the night watch. Later, most boats used a bait mill to grind the bait. (An old Cape Cod joke tells about the fisherman who couldn't fall asleep in his bed at home unless his wife sat beside him and ground a bait mill.)

The fishermen tried to slip alongside of a good-luck vessel, a vessel with a "fishy" skipper. Each man handled two or three lines from stations assigned beforehand, and jerked the flashing silver fish out of the water and snapped them into the barrels with one swift motion.

The mackerel were dressed on board and graded on shore by an official inspector. Then the fish were barreled by young boys, who earned three to five cents a barrel, and sent all over the United States as choice "Massachusetts-inspected" mackerel.

Schooners and Storms

EVERY FISHING VILLAGE counted many widows and orphans among its inhabitants. The coast of Cape Cod, though not rocky, was extremely dangerous, with a double line of hidden sand bars off the "elbow" and not a single harbor before Provincetown out at the very tip. Seafarers depended on steeples, windmills, and beach bonfires to find their way. Lighthouses were few, and the tides, bars, and currents were ever changing. On this wild and hazardous coast the burying grounds were filled with graves that held no bodies, marked by stones that read simply "Lost at Sea."

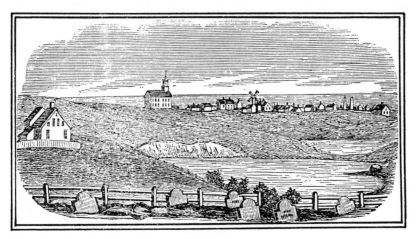

"Chatham" by John Warner Barber.
Society for the Preservation of New England Antiquities.

Just after the Revolution a small private organization
first built huts for shipwrecked men on the lonely beaches of
Cape Cod, "charity houses" equipped with firewood, tinder, and flints to serve as shelters from the fierce blizzards
and sandstorms. (This organization was the ancestor of the
United States Coast Guard.)

Fishermen were no less superstitious than any other mariners. They were dead set against sailing on a Friday.
Marblehead "Bankers" tossed copper pennies on Half-Way
Rock for luck as they went past. Fishermen were discon-
certed by ominous dreams, and some were so upset by birds
that alighted on vessels far from land that they put back
to port immediately. And they took "Jonahs" very seriously. Jonahs were anything or anyone that spoiled their
luck: a man, a dory, a splitting knife.

The Grand Banks was an eerie place of gales, drift ice,
and the dread "summer berg," an icy whiteness plunging
within the dingy whiteness of the fog. The Banks sea was
cold and gray. It "oiled over" sometimes, and grew glassy

and slimy. When the fog dropped without warning, smoking and curling, the fishermen stopped whatever they were doing and heaved up their anchors as the rigging dripped over their heads.

Shuddering, the men spoke of sand walkers and dune haunters and the "yo-hoes" on Monomoy Beach that terrorized lonely clam diggers. The fog bell guided dorymen back to the mother schooners, or perhaps a blast on a conch shell told them where safe refuge waited. Sometimes dories drifted away, unable to find their schooner, and the men lived in dread of bringing up unrecognizable bodies entangled in their lines.

Great gales frequently screamed in off the sea to ravage the coast. The October gale of 1841 destroyed the Sandy Bay breakwater and smashed fourteen schooners in one cove. In that one gale three Cape Cod towns lost eighty-seven heads of families. Five years later the September gale sank eleven Marblehead vessels and killed sixty-five men and boys. The fishing villages had to endure the shock of terrible catastrophes that took the lives of fathers, husbands, brothers, and sons, often within sight of the folk on the shore. Dreadful nightmares haunted the women and children at home. On stormy nights they hardly slept at all, terrified by visions of ships that never returned, as the endless tides rolled over the bones of lost fishermen on the bottom of the sea.

One violent December storm followed a Saturday that had been unusually mild and clear for that time of year. Suddenly the wind veered toward the southeast, and sixty-five coasting schooners and sloops took refuge in Gloucester harbor. The sea was one of the roughest ever seen. People crowded onto the beach and watched helplessly as some

"Shipwreck" by Thomas Birch. *The Brooklyn Museum.*

vessels sank at anchor and others broke loose and smashed on the lee shore. There were twenty wrecks by nightfall, but most of the crewmen of the vessels that went on the rocks were rescued by the hardy fishermen of the village. When the gale died down, thirty damaged vessels were found riding at anchor, and their crews were taken off by a crew of volunteers in the customhouse boat. One vessel, its crew just rescued in the nick of time, drifted out to sea and was never seen again.

On another dark night, a coastal steamer ran down a schooner off Cape Ann. As the schooner went down, a twelve-year-old boy managed to crawl to the end of the bowsprit and cling to a fish-splitting table that went floating by. After crying out frantically, he was finally picked up by the steamer, and then the steamer continued on its way.

Soon afterward, when sails from the schooner washed ashore, the townsfolk gave up all hope. Meanwhile the steamer, by then on its return trip, landed the boy at Eastern Point, about two o'clock in the morning. The lad walked into town and reached his father's house two hours later. He tapped on the window of the ground-floor bedroom.

"Who is there?"

"It's your boy, Winthrop."

The grieving father, half asleep, gasped in horror. But Winthrop, who did not wish to be taken for a ghost, persisted, and soon at the snug cottage there was a great celebration.

One bold young lad, who had heard of the adventures and perils of Georges Bank, was determined to go on a voyage there. The weather was peculiarly mild for February, but none of the superstitious old fishermen could talk him out of the idea. He sailed on schedule, and once on Georges, the cold was intense and the work exhilarating. Some seventy schooners of the fleet lay at anchor, very close to one another.

When the boy hooked his first halibut, the Portuguese steward brought him a mug of hot coffee and a "joe-flogger"—a pancake with plums in it—to celebrate. The fish were so plentiful that the skipper remarked that if their luck held, they would head back in another week. "Georges isn't so bad after all," thought the young fellow.

At sundown, the weather changed abruptly. Clouds massed on the horizon; the wind rose; and the sea grew rough. By eight o'clock the skipper was uneasy.

"Depend on it," said one of the crew. "We're going to have a tough one out of this, and I shouldn't wonder if you had a chance to see more o' Georges than you'll ever want to see ag'in. I've been with the old man half-a-dozen years, and when I see him walkin' and lookin' that way, I make up my mind that somethin's goin' to happen."

The sky was inky black and it was snowing. The lights in each vessel's rigging twinkled as the weary men watched nervously.

"Nap now!"

All but the watch went below. The watch kept a lookout for drifting vessels and paid out ten more fathoms of the anchor cable. By eleven, every plunge of the schooner seemed to be its last, and each man was back on deck, trying to appear calm and cool. The dawn brought a feeling of comfort, but the storm blew on, and the men ate silently while continuing their watch.

Suddenly the skipper cried out, "There's a vessel adrift right ahead of us! Stand by with your hatchet to cut the anchor cable!" The vessel sped toward them and passed so close that the men could see the terror-stricken faces of the crew as they approached certain death. It struck another, and the waters closed over both schooners in an instant.

Two more drifters sped by like phantoms, barely missing the schooner where the young man stood. Yet the gale moderated, and just as if there had been no storm, and no vessels and men had been lost, the crew got their lines ready again, smoking and talking as they worked. They fished through the week, and then the schooner turned homeward. As each vessel limped around Eastern Point the people on shore strained to read her name. All told, fifteen schooners and 120 men were lost in that gale on Georges, leaving seventy widows and one hundred fatherless children in Gloucester alone. The adventurous young man hurried back to his family. "When I got home, they told me I had grown older," he wrote. "I have no wish to try it again."

Cod fishing on the Grand Banks continued through the years in schooners that carried nests of dories on deck, lashed to ringbolts. The sixty-foot main boom divided the deck lengthwise. A tiny galley held pots and pans. Banks skippers took along handbooks of navigation, charts, almanacs, and the sounding line with a lead weight at the end. They smeared the lead with tallow and lowered it to measure the depth of the sea and bring up samples of the ocean bottom. Good skippers got to "think like a cod" as they pondered the nature of the sand, mud, and shells that made up the ocean floor.

The men went out to fish in dories equipped with eight-foot sea oars, small anchors, jugs of water, a horn for signaling, sticks and mauls to stun the fish, lines with leads and hooks, and bait. When they anchored, they signaled with an upended oar, and a man on the schooner waved back to let them know the depth at that spot. Handlining from the dories, the men pulled the cod inboard and wrenched out the hooks. Squid made excellent bait, so at the cry "Squid oh!" the men lowered a piece of lead armed with a circle of pins, and when the squid had wrapped itself around the pins, the men pulled it up. The squid squirted water and ink, and they ended up as black as chimney sweeps.

When the dories returned, the sleepy dorymen bent back and forth to get the kinks out of their bones and ate their supper: a tin pan of cod's tongues with scraps of pork and potato, a chunk of bread, and boiled black coffee cleared with a piece of fish skin.

Then the weary men dressed the cod on deck, by moonlight. Two men stood knee-deep in fish in the cod pen. With a "Hi!" they bent to bring up a fat, three-foot-long cod,

"The Fog Warning" by Winslow Homer.
Courtesy, Museum of Fine Arts, Boston, Otis Norcross Fund.

laid it on the edge of the pen, and slit it open from throat to vent. Another man, his hands protected by mittens, scooped out the liver and dropped it into a basket at his feet. With a second scoop he sent the innards flying and slid the empty fish down the rough table to another man, who split the fish with his curved knife, removed the backbone, and splashed the cod into a tub of water.

"Knife oh!" cried the men from time to time, calling for freshly sharpened knives from the boy. The cook, a strong black man, collected the heads, scraps, and backbones, promising "blood-ends for breakfast, an' head chowder!"

The cleaned fish were pitchforked down the hatch to the hold, where two more men rubbed coarse salt on the ragged

Map of southern New England. (Cape Ann is at the upper right, Cape Cod curves out at the center right, and below it are the islands of Martha's Vineyard, left, and Nantucket, right.)

flesh. The men on deck stopped to drink from the dipper at the scuttle butt forward, and dumped the livers into the "gurry-butt," a cask with a hinged top that was lashed by the forecastle. When the job was done, some of the men rolled straight into their bunks. The others sluiced the cod pen, set up the table to dry, ran the knife blades through a wad of oakum to clean them, and sharpened them on a tiny grindstone.

The cod catch was measured in quintals, or hundred-weights. The first schooner off the Banks full of cod had the right to hoist the "Banks flag." Dories from other vessels came alongside with letters for home, and the fishermen pitched the mail on the deck wrapped around pieces of coal.

Hi! Yi! Yoho! Send your letters round!
All our salt is wetted, an' the anchor's off the ground!
Bend, oh bend your mains'l, we're back to Yankeeland
    With fifteen hundred quintal,
    An' fifteen hundred quintal,
     'Teen hundred toppin' quintal,
'Twixt old 'Quereau an' Grand!

Homeward bound to Gloucester, one fisherman announced his plan to hire a boy to come by his cottage every night and throw water on his bedroom window so that he would be able to drop off to sleep as usual. Restless and impatient, at last the men spied Ten Pound Island and "the Harbor" within its circle of low hills. Through the bayberry bushes they could make out the big red boulders and the fish sheds and the blackened wharves with edges crusted with spilled salt. The first boat in could demand high prices, so all hands waited until their prices were accepted. The catch

was swung ashore in baskets, and the tally was taken as one of the men stood beside the clerk and his scales to check the weights.

Then each fisherman trudged home for a bath and a quiet meal, safely home after another voyage—but never knowing whether his next trip would be his last. It was no wonder that the aged fishermen often spoke reverently of "the port ahead" where, as voyagers to heaven, they would be reunited with the lost friends of a lifetime.

III
Whaling
in the Pacific

So be cheery, my lads, let your hearts never fail,
While the bold harpooner is striking the whale!

Nautical instrument
maker's sign.
*The Whaling Museum,
New Bedford.*

Nantucket and New Bedford

LONG AGO one of the first settlers of Nantucket Island was watching whales spouting offshore. He remarked, "There is a green pasture where our children's grandchildren will go for bread." And so it was—island boys grew up to be whaling captains, and island girls to be shipmasters' wives. The boys of this treeless sandy island, thirty miles out to sea, were soon more at home in the South Seas than in the towns of mainland Massachusetts—if, indeed, they had ever been to the mainland at all!

From the earliest days Yankees had found stranded whales on the beaches, and then ventured out to chase whales in the bays. About 1690, Nantucketers hired an experienced Cape Cod man to teach them the proper way to go a-whaling. Then, in 1712, a Nantucket vessel was carried out to sea in a storm, and chanced to capture an oil-rich sperm whale, a type of whale not found nearer shore. Three quarters of a century later, little Nantucket led the world in whaling. The first whaleship to cross the Equator and the first one to round the Horn were Nantucket vessels, and Nantucket men led the chase after sperm whales into the Pacific Ocean. Only the little Rhode Island schooners known as "plum-pud'ners" continued to hunt the Greenland whale on voyages of only a few months' duration.

Nantucket marketed its own whale products—refined sperm oil and waxy pressed candles. The oil illuminated the streets and homes and lighthouses of the United States and Europe, and the candles, fine and smoke-free, burned with a big flame that gave three times the light of a tallow candle.

In the 1830s the tiny island, with only some eight or nine thousand inhabitants, was the richest community in Massachusetts after Boston and Salem.

"Fairhaven" by John Warner Barber.
Society for the Preservation of New England Antiquities.

Meanwhile the mainland town of New Bedford, with Fairhaven across the harbor, was seriously concentrating on whaling too and, in numbers of ships and men, took the lead away from Nantucket. The poet Emerson noted that in New Bedford, people "hugged an oil cask like a brother." New Bedford fathers gave their daughters whales for dowries when they got married, and it was said that the most dazzling weddings in the nation took place there, for the whaleship owners kept private reserves of the finest grade of oil in their attics to light their lamps on festive occasions.

In summer the streets of New Bedford were canopied by green maples and horse chestnut trees and the houses were as gracious and elegant as any other seaport mansions. But in the whalemen's bethel, or chapel, on Johnny Cake Hill, the mood was always rather sad. Sailors, wives, and widows sat apart from one another, lost in thoughts of loved ones and comrades lost at sea. The chaplain, who had been a harpooner in his youth, wore a blue pilot-cloth jacket and tarpaulin hat, and he addressed his congregation as "Shipmates" from the prow-like pulpit.

On the walls of the bethel were countless tablets in memory of lost whalemen, tablets such as this one:

ERECTED
by the Officers & crew of the
GIDEON HOWLAND
as a token of respect to
SIMEON N. BATES,
of Sandwich, Mass.
1st officer of the ship,
who died July 18, 1839, Æ. 34.
And
WARREN WILBER,
of New-Bedford,
who died Aug. 14, 1839, Æ. 21.

———

Hail brother sailor! whither bound?
What is the course you steer?
Life's various perils press you round,
Dangers and death are near.

Now come about with steady helm,
Thy compass eye with care:
Thy pole-star watch in heaven's realm,
With faith and humble prayer.

Truth's light keep on the starboard bow
Which shines so bright and even:
The spirit's breeze is blowing now,
Fair for the port of heaven.

The search for new whaling grounds took Yankee vessels halfway around the world, and by 1845 New Bedford had ten thousand men a-whaling. Longer voyages called for larger ships, and these larger ships could not easily get to the wharves of Nantucket. Nantucket's inner harbor was blocked by a sandbar, only seven feet below the surface at low tide. Returning whaleships, heavy with oil, had to be floated over the bar on expensive dry docks called "camels" and towed to the wharves. Some vessels had to anchor in the outer harbor and transfer their oil casks to harbor freight boats called lighters. In bad weather ships put in at Martha's Vineyard or a mainland port, usually New Bedford or Fairhaven. But while Nantucket lost her lead in whaling, she never lost her place in the imaginations of people all over the world as "the" home port of the Yankee whaler.

The island was dominated by shrewd, gray-clad Quakers, who grew very wealthy. They cared nothing for frivolous appearances, however, and insisted on a plain, old-fashioned style of dress (though they did not hesitate to use the very best fabrics). The men wore flat "broad-brim" hats and broad-skirted coats, and the ladies wore Quaker bonnets that hid their faces except when seen straight from the front.

These Quakers were not gloomy people, but they favored simplicity of manner. They called one another "Thee" and "Thou" in the familiar way of the Bible, and they gave their children Biblical names such as Peleg, Obed, Shubael, and Keziah. They usually married young, standing up before witnesses and speaking their vows themselves according to Quaker custom. They were extremely serious-minded. They were among the first to speak out against slavery,

"New Bedford Fifty Years Ago" (about 1807) by William A. Wall.
The Kendall Whaling Museum, Sharon, Massachusetts.

quite likely because they had become well acquainted with blacks, Polynesians, and Indians as shipmates and had learned to like and respect men for their characters and skills, no matter what their religious beliefs or skin colors.

They disapproved of swearing, drinking, card playing, and dancing, but they greatly enjoyed parties, where the men swapped whaling stories and the ladies served delicious custards and pies. The older boys and girls and the young married couples attended Wednesday-night reading society meetings regularly. The girls brought their knitting and listened to a serious reading, and later the men came by to read their own compositions, often humorous. The meetings ended with suppers of clam, chicken, or fish chowder, baked beans, and cakes in round and heart shapes.

In summer, parties of merry young people jolted over the bumpy commons in four-wheeled box wagons to Siasconset for a "squantum," or picnic, of crackers and cheese and fresh chowder cooked right on the beach.

Swept by the sea wind, Nantucket was "all beach, without a background." The author Herman Melville had heard it rumored that people there planted toadstools in front of their houses to get under the shade in summertime, and that they were so enclosed and surrounded by the ocean that small clams could sometimes be found adhering to their chairs and tables! The island's only roads were deep-rutted tracks across the common, which was carpeted with low-bush blueberry, dwarf pine, scrub oak, and bayberry. Some of the ruts were so deep that there was no turning back in case of a wrong turn. A wagon just had to keep on going until it came to a "soft place." Thousands of sheep roamed the common, where there was neither a forest nor a farm.

Whale-oil lamp, used at sea.
National Gallery of Art, Index of American Design.

Nantucket sheepshearings were famous, and shearing was the time for family reunions. People came "on from off," onto the island from off on the mainland, from the Cape and the Vineyard and even farther away. The shearings were held on the banks of a large pond each year on "Second and Third days nearest the twentieth of Sixth Month" —the Quaker way of saying Monday and Tuesday nearest the twentieth of June.

The Nantucket wharves had the same busy shipyards, sail lofts, ropewalks, and lumberyards of every seaport town, but there the wharves were lined with establishments that specialized in fitting out whaleships. Coopers were especially important craftsmen. They fashioned oil casks four feet across and five feet high that could hold a ton of sperm oil, shaping the white-oak staves with adzes, drawing them over long planes, and caulking the finished casks with rushes. Coopers took great pride in their touch and their eye, and the apprenticeship was long and difficult. They were held responsible for accurate measurements, and the best of them were highly skilled. An open walk-in hearth was a feature of every cooperage, for the partially formed casks were moistened and placed over a fire of wood shavings to soften and shape them.

The sweet silver sound of the lovely Lisbon bell, brought from Portugal by a Nantucket captain, pealed forth over the harbor from the tower of South Church. Below, innkeepers paved their front yards with clamshells, and served chowder for breakfast, chowder for dinner, chowder for supper. From the heads of the wharves the lanes of the little town meandered up and out into the hills. Once nameless, the streets picked up their names in the most natural way. The alley where someone used to sell cookies became known

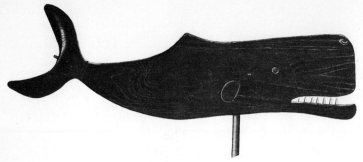

Whale weathervane. *National Gallery of Art,*
Index of American Design.

as Gingerbread Lane, and Step Lane once had steps. A terrible accident must once have happened in Break Neck
Alley. The folk from Polpis used to come into town on Hay
Scale Lane, and pretty New Dollar Lane was named for
the symbol of safe return.

Every captain's home kept a supply of shiny new silver
dollars handy. Island boys competed to be the first to arrive
with the news that a returning ship had been sighted, and
the captain's wife rewarded the winner with one of the new
dollars. The first welcome landmarks of the island for returning whalers were the four windmills high on the hill
west of the town. The windmills were built of ship's timbers, without the use of a single nail. The millers watched
each ship approach until they could decipher the signs of
identification it displayed, revealing the name of its owners
and the size of its cargo of oil, and then they sent the boys
off, running to town. Soon a blue flag with the word SHIP
was run up the flagpole in the center, and everyone who
could spare a few minutes raced up to his "walk" on the
rooftop to watch the vessel come in. In some families, a large
loaf of gingerbread was baked in celebration.

On the rooftops of many houses in the seaports were
railed platforms called "walks" or "captain's walks." These
walks were reached by ship's ladders or steps that led

through a trapdoor next to the large chimney. The walks
themselves were for storing buckets of sand and water to use
in fighting chimney fires. Within the walks there were small
lookout cupolas where spyglasses were kept handy. (Though
many a seafarer's wife searched in vain for a glimpse of her
husband's ship, seaport people did not call these platforms
"widow's walks.")

Most of the island houses had been built by ship carpenters who used housebuilders' handbooks from England as
guides. The carpenters overlapped the sheathing to keep
out the wind and weather, and they used "knees," or beam
brackets, made from the trunks and roots of the white oak
for extra sturdiness. The doorways of the houses were generally Quaker-simple, finely proportioned but not as ornate
as the elegant doorways of Salem.

The parlors of Nantucket and Martha's Vineyard and
New Bedford were filled with treasures from remote Pacific
isles—fishhooks, weapons, feather capes and helmets, paddles, model canoes, bowls, and shells. There were also
Chinese chairs covered in yellow silk, paintings of family

ships, nests of tables, and sewing boxes lacquered crimson and fitted with neat little trays and drawers.

Island schools were better than mainland schools. One academy offered both boys and girls special training in drawing and the projection and coloring of maps, and Nantucket had a special school for master mariners that had been founded by one of its wealthier citizens. Island girls tended to be independent and smart, and several of them grew up to become preachers and mathematicians. One Nantucket girl of twelve helped her father prepare a nautical almanac and make corrections in navigational instruments. She became a noted astronomer and librarian, and sent many an island boy to sea with thorough training in the use of Bowditch's famous book on navigation.

Little children learned ciphering and manners at dame schools, disciplined with a tap on the hand with the pointer or a few hard minutes on the "repentance stool." When children were ready for regular lessons, they learned the three Rs at "cent schools," so called because they cost a cent a day per child. The pupils brought their big copper pennies tied in handkerchiefs or rattling around in their lunch pails. At one school, the children brought their pennies in their mouths and spit them into the same tin cup they all used for drinking water!

Older girls made a little extra money keeping nursery schools for small children a couple of afternoons a week— usually Wednesdays and Saturdays, which were the traditional half days in their own schools.

Women and girls outnumbered men on Nantucket about four to one at any given time, for most of the men were at sea. The ladies entertained one another by going for walks and by visiting, to chat a while over a cup of tea.

Many island wives and widows ran little dry-goods shops, and their daughters helped out regularly by the time they were ten years old. Practical, intelligent Quaker women even took charge of their husbands' business interests while their men were away on three- and four-year voyages. One captain returned after several years at sea and looked over the records his wife had carefully kept for him. Everything was in perfect order and, in his modest and respectful Quaker way he told her simply, "Wife, thee hast done well." It was not surprising that the Quakers were among the first to favor equal rights, especially equal educations, for girls and women.

Every Nantucket youngster, whether rich or poor, learned a trade. One captain, who retired at thirty-seven as a very rich man, made all his daughters learn dressmaking "just in case." The wealthy Joseph Starbuck required his three sons to qualify as master coopers. Then, when the boys got married, he presented each of them with an eighteen-room brick mansion. The "Three Bricks" are almost exactly alike, standing in a row on the upper main street.

Thrifty, hard-headed Nantucketers won their living at a hard and dangerous trade, thousands of miles from home, and they knew better than most men that life had a way of bringing sudden and tragic turns of fortune.

Greasy Whalers

WHALING was never a safe and easy way to make a living, but in the early days many bright young men were attracted by the chance of tremendous profits. Whaling crews were then made up mostly of native-born New Englanders— Yankees, blacks, and Gay Head Indians from Martha's Vineyard. Masters and officers "came in through the hawse hole." They usually knew one another before they went to sea together, and they called the young foremast hands by their first names.

By the 1840s, however, when the American whaling industry reached its peak, there were more than seven hundred vessels and fifteen to twenty thousand men at sea. Whales had become scarcer, and whalemen had to chase their prey in the vast Pacific on voyages of three to four years or even longer. Since the pay for a whaling cruise consisted of shares in the profits, there was no guaranteed wage at all. The pay was higher on merchant and navy vessels, and shoreworkers and factory hands got better pay too. The makeup of the whaling crews changed drastically.

There were only a few experienced seamen in a typical crew of waterfront riffraff and ignorant young farmboys. Drifters, runaways, and stranded foreigners were rounded up and heaved on board the whaleships, often so drunk that they only discovered where they were hours later, their heads pounding and their stomachs churning as the creaking ships pitched and rolled on the sea. Criminals signed on board whaleships, intending to escape the seaport jailers once and for all by jumping ship on some remote South Sea island. No whaleship ever returned with the same crew it had when it started out.

It became so hard to get enough men that the shipping agents asked no questions and put their crews together as fast as they could. Agents traveled from town to town inland, passing out handbills to poor town boys and gullible "hayseeds." These fellows were strong and hardy and used to rising early and working hard, but they dreamed of seeing the world and longed to make quick fortunes. Sick of the dusty streets of Buffalo or the stony hills of Vermont, they were easy marks for the fast-talking agents. And in the seaports, there was little choice of trades, for everything had to do with ships. Many poor town lads were tempted by the promise of a bunk to sleep in every night, with free meals besides.

The agents advertised for "enterprising and industrious young Americans of good moral character"—what boy could resist such a compliment! They promised the boys quick promotions and outfits valued at up to seventy-five dollars. They told of the thrills and sport of whaling and the money to be made—but neglected to mention that if anyone made fortunes whaling, it was the shipmasters and owners.

Oh, the joy of sailing balmy tropic seas for three or four glorious years, the excitement of taking the giant whale, and the barrels of money to bring home! One of the more "trustworthy" agents quickly won the confidence of a Maine farm lad with a sensible-sounding word of caution:

"Now, Hiram," he said, "I'll be honest with you. When you're out in the boats chasin' whales, you git your mince pie *cold!*"

Hiram nodded and gazed absentmindedly out over the pasture. The sweet hay waved gently, and suddenly the old gray barn seemed to arch upward, awesome and mysterious. A white cloud scudded past overhead—or was it a bushy spout? "Bloooows!" mooed the cows from somewhere down by the brook. . . .

The trade winds were blowing softly, and the ship Mermaid *of New Bedford rode easily on the broad Pacific swells. Tall Hiram Smith, just sixteen, was the most famous whaler on the ocean. Pausing at the rail, Hiram graciously accepted a slab of cold but spicy pie from his friend, the ship's cook. Then, pie in one hand and harpoon in the other, he sprang nimbly into the boat.*

"Hurrah!" sang the boat's crew and pulled smoothly away from the ship. . . .

"I'll sign!" cried Hiram.

The agent cleared his throat and shuffled his papers. He

"A Shoal of Sperm Whales off the Island of Hawaii" by Thomas Birch. *Forbes Collection, The Hart Nautical Museum, Massachusetts Institute of Technology.*

promptly arranged for Hiram to be consigned to a large firm in New Bedford, and in a day or two Hiram and a few other boys from his village packed up their belongings and set off for the Pacific.

Hundreds of boys converged on New Bedford and Nantucket, where they were soon pleased to find that generous new friends were on hand to greet them. These "friends" overcharged the bewildered fellows in the boardinghouses, the grogshops, and the outfitters. Occasionally a few of the "greenhands" broke away, and at least one angry farmer rode to New Bedford and took his terrified son straight back to New Hampshire. But most of the boys were too confused to realize what a trap they were in. They loitered in the rundown streets trying to look dashing, but cringing at the sight of a tattooed South Sea Islander in a beaver hat, peddling shrunken heads along the waterfront.

A greenhand got his clothes and bedding free, or at least he paid nothing for them at the time. But the high price was charged against his future earnings, at high interest. He was also charged his share of the ship's insurance, the value of the empty casks, eight or ten dollars for fitting out the ship, a "leakage" charge, and even a dollar or so for the captain's medicine chest.

The captain, who was sometimes part owner of the ship, got a share, or "lay," of about 1/16, the officers 1/25 to 1/35, and the harpooners perhaps as much as 1/20 of the total profits from the sale of the oil. The cooper rated as much as the officers. Ordinary seamen were put down for only 1/150 or 1/165, greenhands for perhaps 1/200, and the cabin boy for as little as 1/250 or 1/300.

At the end of four years of backbreaking labor alternating with terrible boredom, the luckiest greenhand could count on only a few dollars, once all the hidden charges were subtracted from his lay. One harpooner, who signed on at the age of seventeen, cleared only two hundred dollars for four years' work, and wrote in his journal, "Such is fortune." Many a ragged greenhand came home in debt to the owners of the ship. No honest lad ever wanted to ship twice on a whaleship, but a poor boy with no friends or family often had no choice but to ship again and hope to get out of debt the second time around.

Still, there was always the hope of "greasy luck," and whalemen, like all fishermen, traditionally shared bad luck and good. After a bowl of chowder at a waterfront tavern, the greenhands sauntered down to the wharf to have a look at the ship— spotless and shipshape, though a bit broad. The ship's riggers were still hard at work, and would be until the last moment. Picking their teeth with halibut bones, the "greenies" ducked low and entered the forward hatch that led to the crew's quarters. Sixteen to twenty men would share this triangular room in the bow, twelve to sixteen feet across, along with their sea chests and the foremast. No man of average height could stand up straight. A double tier of bunks ran along each side like so many shelves. The only air and light came in through the hatch, which would have to be closed in bad weather. A few oily garments hung from pegs, and in the dimness the boys made out the shapes of several snoring shipmates-to-be.

The fo'c'sle was hot and stuffy, greasy and smoky, and before the vessel even left the lower harbor, the drunks and the greenies would be miserably seasick. In every crew there were a few tough old sea dogs who delighted in teasing the greenhands with horrible tales of vicious whales and cannibals. There were schoolboys, rich men's sons sent to sea to toughen up, gamblers, factory hands, crooks, Kanakas from the South Seas, and one or two mystery men nobody knew anything about at all. There were few married men, and most of the foremast hands were under twenty-one.

In the steerage, below decks amidships, bunked the harpooners or "boatsteerers," some in their late teens or early twenties, perhaps Polynesians or Gay Head Indians from Martha's Vineyard. They were professionals, superior to the foremast hands but socially on good terms with them. They were supposed not to take sides in any dispute between officers and crew. Unlike the foremast hands, they had the run of the ship. The cook, steward, cooper, carpenter, smith, and the cabin boys also bunked in the steerage.

The skippers and officers of Yankee whaleships were on

their own more than those of merchant vessels, which sailed from port to port on a schedule. Whaleships "bound to any ocean" simply followed the whales with no fixed course, and stopped at few civilized ports. The captains could discharge men and recruit new ones, ship their oil home and keep right on whaling, and even sell the ship for a good reason.

Many captains arrived to take command only after the ship was all ready and the entire crew was on board. They were usually capable and proud men, but once on the high seas quite a few of them turned out to be "shore saints and sea devils"—respectable and churchgoing at home but brutal on board ship. They employed strict discipline and harsh punishments to whip their crews into shape, tying disobedient sailors up in the rigging and flogging them publicly as a bitter example to the rest of the men.

Some captains, particularly the Quakers, were deeply religious. They never swore, and on the Sabbath they gathered the men together on deck and read from a large leather-bound Bible, their hands placed on it palms down to keep the pages from fluttering in the wind. Some of these fair-minded captains even gave the men Sundays off, once the essential shipboard duties were done. There were skippers who never took a whale on the Sabbath, although their officers were likely to say privately that when "the old man" sighted a whale on the Sabbath he always knew just where to find it on Monday morning. A shrewd New Bedford shipowner told the mates, "Don't whale it too much a' Lord's days, men, but don't miss a fair chance either— that's rejecting Heaven's good gifts."

Over the years the best whaling captains developed a sort of sixth sense as to where to find the whales. Most of them

Figurehead, "Quaker."
National Gallery of Art,
Index of American Design.

were seasoned skippers by the time they were thirty years old. Whalemen literally lived on the sea. One captain, a-whaling for thirty-seven years, was at home exactly four years and eight months during that period. Another sailed more than a million miles in forty-one years, with a total of only seven years at home in Nantucket. Still another was at home only seventeen months out of fifteen years, and was never present at a family birth or death.

Most skippers and officers were career men from New England, with a thorough knowledge of navigation and a confidence based on experience. Few had any formal medical training, but they all knew something about treating accidents and illness. Crewmen sometimes fell from a hundred feet up in the rigging, from dizziness, seasickness, or carelessness. A "stove boat," one smashed to splinters by a whale, was so frequent an accident that it was entered without comment in the logbook unless a life was lost. A fall into the sea was far less serious than a fall onto the hard deck. Men suffered serious injuries while stowing heavy casks in the hold. Toothaches were common, and the cure was simple: the captain or the mate held the victim's head back against a coil of rope and yanked out the tooth with a handy "claw." The wound usually healed all right, and on board a whaleship one could not be too upset if a few splinters of jawbone came out with the tooth.

Among the crew on every whaleship there were likely to be free black men—natives of New England seaports as well as blacks from Portuguese Cape Verde off the coast of Africa. Blacks made superior whalers, and there were even a few black captains who commanded ships with all-black crews. Kanakas from the South Sea islands also made good whalers. Strong and cheerful, they were excellent swimmers besides, and were much admired by the Yankees, many of whom could not swim a stroke.

The cabin boy, youngest member of the crew, assisted the steward in setting the table for the captain's and the officers' meals and in washing the dishes, fed the pigs and chickens that were often carried to supply fresh meat, ran errands, took messages forward, and brought the captain his charts. Cabin boys were often the special pets of the crew. Some boys, ambitious and quick to learn, managed to master the essentials of seamanship—making knots, furling sails, rigging, and rowing, and taking their turn at the helm.

Foremast hands were called by their first or last names. The cooper, carpenter, steward, and smith were addressed as such, and the cook was "Doctor." The officers were

"Mr. ——," and the captain was "Sir." The cabin boy was usually just "Boy," and sometimes the crew never even knew his name.

All hands took along their own jackets, pants, shirts, shoes and stockings, underwear, bedding, needles and thread, soap, razor, jackknife, tin plate, and spoon. Whalers would do anything to get the last bit of use out of their clothes, which were often little more than holes pieced together by scraps. Merchant sailors, snappy in their bell-bottoms and checked shirts and shiny black hats, scorned whalemen, who were anything but smart in their pants of brown or gray or green, complete with suspenders and pockets—the garb of a landsman.

There was no way for a whaler to get spending money for shore leaves except by buying articles from the captain's "slop chest" and selling them in port. Whalers (and merchant sailors too) replaced their worn-out clothing and bought their tobacco from these shipboard stores. Purchases were charged against their accounts at half again their true value, and deducted from their lays, or wages, at the end of the voyage. The slop chests held plenty of printed cottons and trinkets to sell to the South Sea islanders, and the ships' account books were filled with curious entries. One foremast hand charged nine pounds of tobacco, one box of soap, ten yards of denim cloth, and two birds of paradise. A boatsteerer on the same ship bought six yards of printed cotton, a straw hat—and one finger ring!

Since whaleships cruised for years, far from established sea lanes, wherever the rumor of whales led them, they carried supplies for every possible emergency. It was very expensive to equip a whaleship for such a long voyage. The ship took on food and water, barrel staves in bundles,

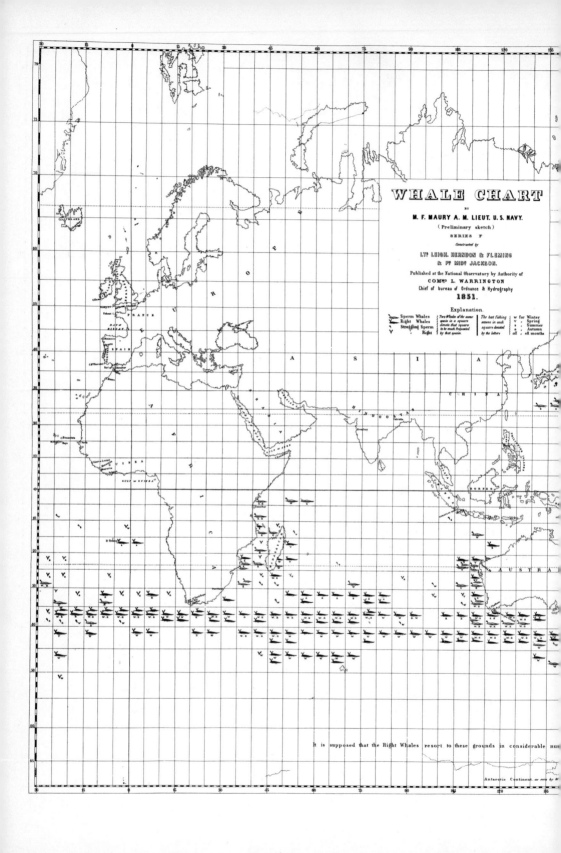

Unexplored by Whalemen.

...od fishing may be had in these latitudes during winter (w) i. e. the Southern Summer.

chains, anchors, iron hoops, black iron try-pots—for boiling down whale blubber into oil—bricks, nails, fishhooks, harpoons and lances, knives, instruments, charts, almanacs, spyglasses, lumber, spare boats, oars, masts, yards, block and tackle, cordage and lines, paint and turpentine, bolts of canvas, sails, flags, tools, hardware, medicines, lamps, candlesticks, candles, washbasins, pots and pans, spoons, ladles, kegs, needles, crockery, quill pens and logbooks—spare everything, almost, except a spare captain and ship.

The main hold was filled with hundreds of oil casks of various sizes. Outward bound, many in the lowest tier were filled with fresh water, and many in the upper tier held the provisions and supplies that would be used first, emptying the casks for the first batches of oil. The forehold was jammed with spare rigging, hawsers, anchors, lumber, and gear for cutting up the whales' blubber.

Tremendous quantities of foodstuffs were loaded aboard —a hundred barrels each of salt beef and pork, tons of hard bread and flour, molasses, salt fish, potatoes, rice, beans, corn, dried apples, tea, and coffee. Until the 1830s, when the temperance movement put a stop to it, all vessels took along plenty of rum for grog to warm the poor wet sailors. And naturally, there was butter, white sugar, vinegar, pickles, and a jar of homemade jam—for the cabin.

Whaleships were built for great capacity, not for speed. Since they were seldom going anywhere in particular, they were seldom in a hurry. Their timbers soaked with oil, their sterns square, the lumbering vessels were anything but beautiful. Merchant seamen jeered that "spouters" were built by the mile and simply sawed off in lengths. They insisted that a good nose could smell a dingy old "blubber boiler" twenty miles to windward.

The whaleships were often surprisingly small—perhaps only 130 feet long—but the decks were broad and roomy, and the planking was thick enough to weather the heaviest storm and to protect the ship if it ever ran aground. These stout ships were usually square-rigged with three masts, and had a white "waistband" painted with imitation gunports to scare away pirates. American whaleships had several unique features. The most striking was the "tryworks" on the deck with its two iron pots set in a solidly built brick furnace braced and screwed down on especially stout deck timbers. The tryworks was sheltered from rain, snow, and sleet by its own scorched "house" overhead.

High on the mastheads there were tiny platforms for the lookouts, with iron hoops at about waist-height, nailed to the mast, to support the lookout's arms.

On wooden cranes or davits at the sides hung the whaleboats, three on the larboard, or port, side and one on the starboard side, leaving room for the gangway and the cutting platform that was lowered over the captured whale. Between the main and mizzen masts two or three spare boats were stored bottoms up, and cast a nice patch of shade over the captain's cabin.

The six-man whaleboats, as graceful as the ships were stubby, were so light and fragile that two men could lift one, and yet they were the most seaworthy boats ever known. They were double-ended, like their Viking ancestors and like the modern surf lifeboat. They were twenty-six to twenty-eight feet long, slender, and equally fast in either direction. The boatheader steered from the stern with an oar as long as the boat itself, and the five other oarsmen sat alternating on either side.

Each whaleboat carried a mast and small sail, oars,

paddles, harpoons and lances, sealed kegs of water and of bread, a keg of survival gear (candles, tinder, flints, steel, and a lantern), and tubs of line. The line, of best quality tarred hemp, was coiled in the tub with extreme care, for one kink in a flying line attached to a harpooned whale could tear off a man's arm or leg, or whip him out of the whaleboat and into the sea. |

The Chase

THERE! She blows! There! There! There! She blows! BLOOOOOWS!" sang the lookout, a hundred feet above the deck. In the distance a whale had just exhaled, and its warm breath created a bushy spout in the cooler air.

"There! She blooooows!"

The skipper sprang into the rigging and scanned the horizon with his spyglass. "Where away?"

"Two points off the lee bow, sir, scarce three miles away!"

"Way down from aloft! Call all hands, Mr. Russell," bellowed the captain to the mate.

The watch below had already heard the commotion and raced abovedecks. The greenhands were tremendously excited at their first sight of whales breaching. The giant creatures leaped two thirds their own length into the air and landed on their backs with ear-splitting cracks. Some of the whales were "lobtailing"—standing on their heads and beating the sea with their "flukes," or tails—and others were sliding down from the crests of waves and spouting lazily in the hollows.

"Lower away boats!" Within minutes after the whales had been "raised," four whaleboats, six oarsmen in each, had splashed into the water. When the captain himself commanded one of the boats, the ship was left under shortened sail in charge of the cooper, carpenter, cook, steward, and boy.

"Out oars! Use great care so as not to gally them!" cried the captain, for whales were easily "gallied," or frightened.

The boats sped toward the prey as quietly as possible, because whales' tiny ears are very keen. The men put up a small sail if the whales were to leeward, and they went barefoot in warm weather—that was quieter too. They switched to paddles to approach even more silently. The mother vessel, in its own code, signaled with sails and flags to inform the men in the boats about the location and activities of the whales.

"There go flukes!" sang out the mate. Some of the whales, alerted to danger, had submerged. Whales could submerge, or "sound," up to an hour, so the men had to rest their oars and wait. The gallied whales sped away, usually to windward. They could swim all day long, never varying so much as a compass point from their course.

"Roar and pull, boys! Beach me on their black backs, boys!" coaxed one of the mates from the stern of his whaleboat. "Why don't you snap your oars, you rascals? That's it, long and strong! Pull, will you? Pull, can't you? Keep cool, keep cool—cucumbers is the word. Only pull! Do that for me and I'll give you my house, boys, and my wife and children, boys! PULL!"

The mate cursed and begged, and the men had to follow his orders without question. Only the mate, facing forward and acting as "boatheader," could actually see how close they were coming to the whales, for the other men faced the stern. It was an unwritten rule that the oarsmen were never, never, to turn around to look at the awesome prey. Panicky greenhands had to be knocked out promptly with a blow on the head—they would be no use, but no trouble either.

Experienced whalemen could detect the seaweedy smell of the monstrous creatures without even looking over their shoulders. They were very near. Suddenly the mate whispered, "Stand up and give it to him!"

The boatsteerer in the bow, already exhausted from rowing for hours, shipped his long oar, leaped up, grabbed his harpoon with both hands, braced his thigh hard against the gunwale, turned, and hurled the iron at the whale. The barbed weapon, marked with the name of ship and master, hissed forward, with a one-in-ten chance of striking.

"He's fast! Stern all, stern all, for your lives!" The oars seemed to bend as the men frantically backwatered to get out of the way of the whale's powerful flukes. The whale, in anguish, threw itself out of the water, and the sea heaved as if the whole earth had quaked. Then the whale took off, and the men were on a "Nantucket sleigh ride" in spray and foam, when the slightest shift of balance would mean disaster. The boat skimmed and thumped on the tops of the waves, and one of the oarsmen scooped sea water up in his hat to douse the smoking-hot line that whizzed out of the boat between the men sitting on either side.

Even as the boat began its whirlwind ride, the boatsteerer, having placed his harpoon, had rushed to the stern to take the place of the mate at the steering oar and tend the line attached to the harpoon that stuck fast in the whale, all the while trying to keep the boat from capsizing.

"The Capture" by Benjamin Russell, after drawings by A. Van Beest and R. S. Gifford. *Forbes Collection, The Hart Nautical Museum, Massachusetts Institute of Technology.*

At the same moment, the mate had run forward to take his new stand in the bow, poised to kill the whale with a lance!

The whale rushed on, perhaps for miles. He might sound so deeply that the men would have to cut the line to avoid being dragged under themselves. The furious animal rolled over and over with incredible speed, thrashed the sea with his flukes, ran his head out of the water, and snapped his jaws together. At any time, he might turn on the boat and bite it in two. But at last, if all went well, the great whale tired.

"Haul in, haul in!" The men pulled hand over hand on the wet line, coiling it loosely in the stern, until they came up close to the whale. Even then, a sly "sparm" could rear up under the boat and deliberately smash it like an eggshell.

For the kill, the mate, now in the bow, pushed the lance repeatedly into the whale's hump, trying to reach the "life," the one thin vulnerable spot in the whale's body. Each thrust opened up new wounds. The sea reddened, and hot spray from the spouthole showered the men in the boat.

Then the lance struck the "life," and the whale's lungs were flooded with his own blood. His "chimney afire," the dying beast entered his hideous "flurry." Clashing his jaws, he rushed in ever narrowing circles. Blood gushed forth as the suffocating whale rolled feebly from side to side. At last, his huge heart burst and he turned "fin out." Every whale circled one final time and held its head toward the sun at the moment of death.

Shaken by the awful sight, and dead tired besides, the men cut a hole in the flukes and put a line around the narrowest part of the tail to tow the dead whale back to the ship. The ship could sail to the prize only if the wind blew in the direction of the whale. Many a boat's crew had to tow a whale for miles in a gale or in the blackness of night, and it was extremely dangerous to secure the carcass alongside the ship in rough seas.

Then, no matter what the hour, the "cutting in" and "trying out" began immediately. The "cutting stage," a frail plank platform, was lowered over the starboard rail. It hung fifteen or twenty feet out from the side. There the officers stood while making cuts for the blubber hook and slicing into the blubber with razor-sharp cutting spades.

"Overboard hook!"

A rope around his waist, one of the boatsteerers stood on the slippery whale and secured the hook in a cut. The blubber, the whale's insulation from the cold and pressure of the deep sea, was tough and elastic and as much as two feet thick. Gulls screamed, and sharks snapped at the men's feet. The whale rolled ponderously as the first "blanket piece" of blubber peeled away and was lifted clear and swung up over the gangway.

Each piece, weighing a ton or more, was caught by a second hook at the lower end and passed through the hatch to the blubber room below. The ship rolled sharply to one side from the weight, and the swinging blanket piece nearly sent one of the men spinning off the slanting deck into the shark-filled sea. Down in the blubber room two men, soaked with oil, cut the blubber into square "horse pieces" and passed them back on deck. These pieces were minced with two-handled cleavers into thin "books" or "Bible leaves" that were tossed into the try-pots to be boiled until the oil separated from the fibers.

The mates and boatsteerers tended the fires. A trough of seawater kept the decks from catching fire. All hands worked day and night, and only the cook was free to do his regular work or mix up a batch of doughnuts to fry in the try-pots. Some of the men dipped pieces of hardtack in the

"Trying Out in the Night" by Benjamin Russell. *Forbes Collection, The Hart Nautical Museum, Massachusetts Institute of Technology.*

oil and chewed on them. The fires were fed with scraps of tried-out blubber, and evil-smelling smoke billowed up and blackened the sails. While the officers ladled the oil into the copper cooler and then into wooden casks, the men in the main hold worked to stow away the heavy, oily casks at the risk of being crushed with every roll of the ship.

The deck ran with "gurry," a sickening mess of blood and seawater and grease and bits of whale meat. The ship was a vision of hell, hissing and flaming on the surface of the mysterious ocean. Although the men felt cold and clammy, their eyes burned from the smoke as they groped their way to the rail for a breath of cleaner air. Their clothes were drenched with salt water and oil. They were almost too exhausted to notice the blisters that swelled their bare feet.

The mates severed the head, fully a third of the whale's length, and hoisted it on board to cut it apart. (If the head was unusually large, it was cut apart while lashed to the side.) If the whale was a toothless right whale, the men removed the long thin slabs of tough "baleen," or whalebone, the lengths of hornlike material in the whale's mouth. Right whales fed on tiny plankton, or "brit," scooping up great gulps of sea water and trapping their food within the baleen as they let the water drain out the sides of their mouths. The right whale's tongue, almost pure fat, was also cut out.

If the whale was a sperm whale, one of the men stood in the upper part of the head, or "case," up to his waist in colorless oil as clear as water, and bailed out the sweet liquid. The whale's lower forehead, or "junk," contained grainy, waxy, spongy spermaceti, delicate and pinkish, that was used to make fine-quality candles.

The men plunged cutting spades into the carcass of the sperm whale, hoping to find the rarest and most valuable treasure of all: ashen-colored ambergris, spongy and rubbery. Ambergris was found only in the intestines of sick sperm whales, and the great lumps contained undigested parrotlike beaks of the hideous giant squid on which the sperm whales fed in the depths of the ocean. Ambergris was not heavily scented itself, but it absorbed other scents and was used in expensive perfumes. A couple of hundred pounds of ambergris, at two to four hundred dollars a pound, was worth more than a whole shipful of oil.

Hours, even days, passed. The surface of the sea around the ship was slicked smooth by oil leaking from the body of the whale. At last all the blubber had found its way into the try-pots, so the carcass was set adrift for the sharks to tear apart. The lower jaw of the sperm whale was left to rot on deck until the ivory teeth could be pulled out.

The men mopped the decks and polished them with sharkskin until they glistened. They scrubbed the rails and polished the try-pots and put the hatches back over the try-works. Only the sails would never be white again. Finally the men washed and changed their clothes. They took out their tobacco and smoked for a moment in silence, wondering what the next few hours would bring, for more whales were all that mattered. The lookout at the masthead started, raised his head and narrowed his eyes.

"There! She blows! BLOOOOWS! BLOOOOOOWS!"

Bound to Any Ocean

THE FIRST DAYS OUT on a whaling voyage were a misery of seasickness for the greenhands. Some captains were sympathetic, but most of them ordered all hands on deck the first day out, seasick or no. The men were divided into two watches that would stand duty for four hours and then go below for four. And the mates chose their boat crews.

The skipper stalked the deck and made a little speech outlining the rules of the ship and pointing out the need for hard work. He promised fair treatment for good behavior and effort. Otherwise, watch out!

During the first weeks the greenhands had to be broken in. The officers bullied the hayseeds and the waterfront bums into the rigging with curses and kicks, and taught them to scrub the decks, make knots, and paint. The greenies lived through their most horrible nightmare: the climb aloft to the lookout with the ship pitching and rolling, the motion doubling and tripling the higher they inched. They took their "trick" at the wheel, a queasy job even in fair weather. Over and over they practiced lowering the boats, rowing with the long oars, and paddling soundlessly without touching the sides of the boat, and they learned to reverse oars instantly at the mate's command.

In the first storm, while forty-foot waves crashed over the decks and seawater oozed through the fo'c'sle walls, the greenies huddled in their bunks, wrapped in greasy blankets, with seagoing rats for company, and listened to the swish of the sea and the groaning of the ship's joints.

The food on board a whaleship was not exactly what country boys were used to, and very often there wasn't even enough of it. They soon agreed that "God sends meat, but the devil sends cooks," for the cook on a whaleship was seldom trained for his job. He threw the food together and ladled it out into tubs, or "kids"—one for the salt meat and one for potatoes or vegetables, if there were any. The crew ate their stringy "salt junk" and ship's biscuit on deck in fair weather and in the forecastle in bad weather, dishing out their share with jackknives or fingers into their own tin plates. They got a bucket of coffee every morning and weak tea every evening—the tea and coffee, sweetened with sour molasses, were useful for soaking worms out of the hardtack.

On one vessel the dull daily meal was "lobscouse," a stew of hardtack and "top-of-the-pot" (the grease left from boiling salt beef or pork) boiled up with a little molasses. When the crew began to talk about mutiny, the cook dreamed up "potato scouse," which substituted potato for the grease. There were always plenty of splinters and bits of rope in his concoctions. Eventually the hardtack grew so full of maggots that one seaman swore it walked across the deck all by itself.

One ship took several hundred chickens on board when it stopped at an island in the South Pacific. The cook boiled the leathery birds and tossed one apiece into the mess kid. The chicken dinner was so bad that the men sent a delegation to the captain to demand the "salt horse" they had been promised when they shipped.

If a pig was slaughtered on board, the roast pork appeared only in the cabin, and the forecastle got a little pork soup. Any flying fish that landed on deck were destined for the captain's table. On Sundays there was sometimes a boiled pudding, and on certain ships it was the custom for the cook to fry up a batch of doughnuts for every thousand

barrels of oil. Old hands smacked their lips over whale's
lips and brains. If there had been any time to catch a few
fresh fish, the old fellows revolted the greenhands as they
devoured mugfuls of fish innards, baked or raw.

All ships had to make occasional stops to take on fresh
water and provisions, for without greens, onions, potatoes,
and other vitamin-rich foods seamen developed scurvy, a
painful swelling of faces, hands, and feet. Luckily scurvy
could be quickly cured with fresh vegetables and fruit.
Most whalers made their first stop at the Azores—the
Western Islands—or the Cape Verde Islands in the Atlantic. The boys were always delighted at the sight of the green
islands with their tall peaks and whitewashed towns.

At Fayal one of the whaleboats made several trips ashore
for eggs, oranges, potatoes, onions, and chickens. The captain went off to mail a few letters and hire a few "Portygee"
recruits. In the harbor he ran into his brother, also a whaling captain, whom he had not seen for sixteen years—they
had never happened to be home in New Bedford at the
same time.

After all the provisions were aboard, the captain allowed
one boatsteerer—a lad of seventeen—to take several of the
greenhands ashore on liberty for the morning. He gave the
boatsteerer a dollar and told him to take the boys somewhere for lunch before meeting the third mate to return to
the ship.

The youngsters ambled around the dusty streets until
they found a place that looked pretty clean. Inside the
restaurant, the distinguished-looking Portuguese host show-
ed them to a table decked with luscious fruit and beautiful flowers. He set out a round of glasses and a carafe of
red wine, and then brought in a brimming platter of fra-

"Fayal" by an unknown artist.
The Kendall Whaling Museum, Sharon, Massachusetts.

grant stewed chicken and sauce. The Yankee boys thought they had never been so hungry in their lives. But they took one bite and dropped their forks—garlic! They did eat their fill of the fresh fruit, and the bill, written in script on a piece of yellow paper a yard long, came to exactly seventy-five cents.

Sailors and whalers held a ceremony of initiation for those who were crossing the Equator for the first time. One whaleship neared "the Line" early in the evening. The greenhands were solemnly informed that Old Neptune, who

"Panorama of a Whaling Voyage" by Thomas F. Davidson.
Courtesy of the Peabody Museum of Salem.

never let a whaleman pass through his empire without stopping him, was due on board. While the captain teased the greenhands at the helm, the other crewmen shook their heads and made mysterious remarks. The nervous greenies were then sent below, and the hatch was shut and guarded.

The rest of the men quickly set up a large blubber tub on deck and filled it to the brim with salt water. They rigged up an arrangement of tubs and boards, banging the deck as hard as they could, while the greenies cowered below. The mate dressed up in an old jacket and put on whiskers of manila yarn and spun yarn "seaweed" for hair. He took a pronged harpoon in one hand and an old speaking trumpet in the other, mounted to the bowsprit, and bellowed:

"Ship ahoy!"

"Hello!" answered the captain.

"What ship is that?"

"Ship *Spouter*, New Bedford."

"Have you any subjects for me?"

The captain motioned to the crew to tramp loudly on the deck to scare the greenhands all the more. Neptune came down to the deck and sat on an overturned scrap tub.

"Bring on the youngsters. I am in a hurry!"

The first greenhand was summoned, blindfolded, and led over to Old Neptune. He was ordered to answer Neptune's questions at once, but every time he opened his mouth to speak he got a tar brush in his face. The men lathered his face with grease and soft soap, and "shaved" him with a piece of hoop iron.

"Can you swim?" Old Neptune inquired.

Before the greenhand could reply, the men threw a bucket of water in his face and tipped him up and slid him head over heels into the big tub.

"Man overboard!"

The terrified greenhand frantically paddled a stroke—and his hands bumped the edge of the tub. He tore off his blindfold, furious and humiliated, while the rest of the men collapsed on the deck with laughter. One by one, they brought out all the greenies, teased them about their quirks and their girl friends, and dunked them in the water, until all were initiated as true subjects of old sea-god Neptune.

Months passed uneventfully on whaleships on their way to the Pacific cruising grounds. The crew sharpened harpoons and lances and cutting spades and fitted them to poles, checked the boats and oars, coiled the lines, and patched their clothes. The morning watch scrubbed the deck every day before breakfast. And since there never

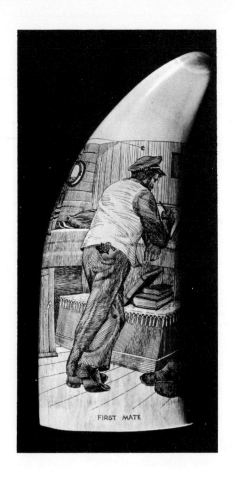

FIRST MATE

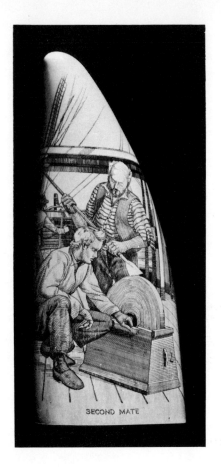

SECOND MATE

was a whaleship that didn't leak a little, they manned the pumps. (Thrifty New Bedford Quakers bought up quite a few old merchant ships after Salem's foreign trade declined, including one ship that had been used in the Sumatra trade. On her first voyage as a whaleship, the men brought up pepper every time they manned the pumps.)

Sails had to be checked and patched after squalls, but there was no need constantly to adjust the sails for maximum speed on the cruising grounds. For days at a time, various kinds of fish would accompany the slow-moving whaleships. A school of "porps" tumbling and clowning off

Three whale's teeth
(scrimshaw).
Courtesy,
The Mariners Museum,
Newport News, Virginia.

the bow was hailed with delight, for sailors considered them lucky. The porpoise is a member of the whale family; in fact, it is a sperm whale in miniature. Porpoises yielded little oil, but their meat was good. (As always, however, the choicest parts—liver, brains, and kidneys—appeared only on the cabin table.)

The usual course of a whaleship on a voyage to the Pacific was to spend a while in early summer north of the Sandwich Islands (Hawaii), then to cruise northward and on to the Japan whaling grounds in the fall. In the winter the ship circled down off the coast of California, down the west coast of South America, and back across the South Pacific. In the spring the ship sailed northward again, cruised six months or so, and then went on westward, possibly to the China Sea and Samoa, back eastward "on the Line." A ship could cruise all year round on the "offshore grounds" along the Equator near Peru and Chile.

Once around Cape Horn, whaleships headed for the Galápagos Islands. There the men went ashore to capture the giant tortoises, four feet long with domed shells, that would provide fresh meat for the ship. The tortoises could live on board for up to a year without food or water and without losing weight, and the old seamen told the greenies they were reincarnated sea captains.

Every whaleship stopped at the "whaleman's post office" on Santa Maria Island in the Galápagos—a mailbox (at first, just a tortoise shell) nailed to a tree. There the men left letters addressed simply to "—— ——, Boatsteerer, Ship——, Pacific Ocean." Homeward-bound vessels stopped to pick up letters that were two or three years old but still more precious than gold.

On the cruising grounds there were many idle and monotonous hours. Dead calms could last for as long as a month, and the men could not sleep in the tropic heat. The steady shine of the sun dulled the men's spirits, and days and weeks passed with growing tension. The sails hung limp, and the men had to wet down the decks to keep from burning their bare feet. The men at the lookouts grew dizzy, and their eyes ached from the glare of the sun on the glassy sea. The crew retarred the seams of the deck, wet down the oil casks so they would not shrink and leak, and filled the whaleboats with water to keep them tight. And they saw how the hogs crowded into the shade, and doused them with sea water, and laughed at the happy squeals of the porkers.

The men suffered fits of homesickness, and if no whales were sighted, they grumbled and quarreled, and the officers grew harsh and short-tempered. After weeks of depression, a captured whale was cause for a great celebration, and possibly a surprising break in the usual shipboard discipline. When a teen-age boatsteerer on a hard-luck voyage struck a huge "120-barrel" whale, the captain even invited him to the cabin for a drink of whiskey and called him by his nickname!

Many crewmen kept journals. They drew pictures and wrote sentimental poems and complained about the food, and ten thousand miles from home, they carefully noted family birthdays and anniversaries.

The first mate kept the logbook, the official record of the voyage for the shipowners, starting the sea day at noon and recording wind, weather, latitude, longitude, and often much more. The logbook recorded whales caught or lost, using different wooden stamps carved by the whalemen themselves. There were stamps to signify sperm whales, right whales, porpoises, and "flukes" for whales lost. The mates stamped the marks in black or blue ink, sometimes painting in blood-red spouts. Some stamps had blank spaces in the whale's body for entering the number of barrels of oil by hand.

The logbook also contained records of accidents, deaths, and burials at sea, with black lines carefully drawn around that day's entry. The captain or mate read the burial service; the ship's bell tolled; the body, sewn in canvas, was slid into the sea; and the man's few possessions were auctioned off to the rest of the crew.

Each day's entry ended with the words "So ends this day," or just "So ends" or "So ends & c."

Many a logbook noted "all hands employed in scrimshawing"—polishing and decorating whale's teeth. It was the unique hobby of the American whalemen. By an unwritten rule the four- or five-inch teeth of the sperm whale belonged to the crew. The men spent hours polishing and filing the rough, ribbed teeth on the ship's grindstone or with hand files, rubbing them with sharkskin or ashes from the tryworks, and smoothing them with the palms of their hands. Usually with nothing but their jackknives, they etched their designs in the ivory and darkened the lines with ink or soot or "gunk and gurry" from the tryworks. They drew original scenes of ships and whaling or transferred pictures from newspapers and books.

Most of the men made carved gifts for their wives and sweethearts and mothers, and were fondest of making "jagging wheels," tools for crimping piecrust and pastry, many of them very ornamental with little forks at one end. The sailors also made birdcages, needlecases, napkin rings, letter openers, umbrella handles, jackstraws, chessmen, dominoes, handles for dippers of coconut shell, cane heads, spool racks, bracelets, collapsible "swifts" for holding skeins of knitting yarn, boxes inlaid with bits of shell and rare wood, and corset stays with romantic verses inscribed on them. The men enjoyed inscribing whale's teeth with such mottoes as "To our wives and sweethearts, may they never meet" and "Death to the living, long life to the killers, success to sailors' wives, and greasy Luck to whalers."

Whalemen were lonely, enduring months and even years without a single line of news from home. Their special delight was the "gam," a social get-together of two or more

S. Boat.	L. Boat.	W. Boat.
May 24th 1854.	July 5th 1854.	Dec. 12th 1854.
B. 40 bbls.	B. 25 bbls.	B. 55 bbls.
Nov. 4th 1854.	Oct. 20th 1854.	Dec. 9th 1855.
B. 35 bbls.	B. 45 bbls.	B. 70 bbls.
Oct. 17th 1855.	Oct. 26th 1855.	May 11th 1856.
B. 45 bbls.	B. 30 bbls.	C. 10 bbls.
May 11th 1856.		May 14th 1856.
C. 30 bbls.		C. 30 bbls.
June 13th 1856.		
C. 25 bbls.		
Jany. 6th 1857.		
B. 70 bbls.		
Jany. 20th 1857.		
B. 65 bbls.		
Jany. 28th 1857.		
B. 60 bbls.		
Feby. 1st 1857.		
B. 60 bbls.		

whaleships that met on the cruising grounds. One ship hauled up its mainsail to invite the other ship to have a gam, and the second ship did the same to accept.

"Ship ahoy!"

"What ship is that?"

"Ship *Martha*, Nantucket."

"How long are you out, and with what success?"

"Fourteen months, and eight hundred barrels of oil!"

A gam might last several hours or overnight, and sometimes several ships cruised together for a week or so. A gam was especially nice when the captains came from the same home port. If both ships had been out for some time there was little news, but there were usually acquaintances on board both ships. A gam was a holiday, with plum duff and a round of grog for all.

Traditionally the skippers and their boat crews visited on one vessel, and the mates and their boat crews on the other. The visiting captain was rowed across to the other ship in the starboard boat, standing erect as a pine tree and never holding on, no matter how rough the sea—it was a point of honor and he tried to keep his dignity, for the crews of both vessels were watching. Wedged in before and behind, hands in his pockets, he was whacked in the knees by the oars, while the long steering oar slammed him in the back.

Whaleships outward bound always took along letters and newspapers for other ships known to be cruising the same waters, so there were often bulletins from home. What matter if the letters were months old and the papers thumbworn, when all the papers on board were two *years* old.

The crew swapped books, borrowed needles and thread, and exchanged souvenirs. They shared smokes and danced and sang with their new friends. A favorite song was:

I asked a maiden by my side,
　Who sighed and looked at me forlorn,
"Where is your heart?" She quick replied,
　" 'Round Cape Horn."

I said, "I'll let your father know,"
　To boys in mischief on the lawn;
They all replied, "Then you must go
　'Round Cape Horn."

In fact, I asked a little boy
　If he could tell where he was born;
He answered, with a mark of joy,
　" 'Round Cape Horn."

There was a cheerful rivalry in yarns and curses if one ship was a "sound boat" from New Bedford and the other an "island vessel." The sailors spun yarns for hours and hours—wild stories about girls in foreign ports, the paradise islands of the South Seas, and tales of "stove" boats, cannibals, and mutinies.

"Have ye seen Mocha Dick?" they always asked. The great ferocious white whale who hunted whalemen and bit their boats in two, the old scarred bull, intelligent and evil, had been seen in various parts of the world at the very same time—in the South Atlantic, the Pacific, off Japan, off Chile. He was the malevolent deathly-white whale, half real, half ghost. "Have ye seen Mocha Dick?" they whispered.

One whaling captain, gamming with another captain from his own home port, received the terrible news that one of his three children had died since he sailed away. But the second captain could not remember which one. The grieving father suffered many months of agony, wondering which of his beloved children he would never see again.

At Home at Sea

WHALING WIVES at home, too, lived through years of loneliness without their husbands. They gave birth to babies alone, and sometimes saw those babies sicken and die—to their absent fathers it was just as if they had never lived at all. Many wives decided that anything, even the hardships and dangers of a "greasy voyage," was better than staying home alone. They packed up their children and resolved to set up housekeeping in the cramped, poorly ventilated cabin of a whaleship.

Cramped as it was, the cabin was often a miniature version of a New England cottage, furnished with a rocker or a horsehair sofa and a pot of geraniums. The captain and his wife slept in a bed that swung on gimbals that kept it level even in rolling seas, under a patchwork quilt from home, and with just a small chest of drawers and a washstand crammed into the little room off the cabin. A compass hung over the bed, and another hung over the table where the family and the officers ate, a table with little railings to keep the dishes from sliding off onto the floor. Off the small dining saloon were staterooms for the officers—one for the mate and another, with bunks, for the lesser officers.

Seagoing children expected adventure, but what they got, most of the time, was dull food, no friends to play with, and lessons every day but Sunday. One brother might be an ordinary seaman, another the cabin boy, but the youngest children occupied the cabin with their parents. The first problem was seasickness. One three-year-old felt the deck sinking away underfoot and announced that he felt bad all over. He threw up, fell asleep, and woke up feeling fine. His

"Mrs. John Harrison and Her Daughter Maria" by Nathaniel
Mayhew. *Collection of Edgar William and Bernice Chrysler Garbisch.*

poor mother, unfortunately, was seasick all the first week,
and again after every stay in port.

Mothers worried about accidents, especially with no doctor on board, but the children did not seem to care so much.
One boy, five years old, went ashore on a tropic island with
the mate, to buy some potatoes. On the way back the boat
overturned, but the boy wasn't the least bit frightened. He
raced down to change his clothes and go right back again,
and he was furious when his mother said "No!"

Another boy, who loved the voyage, fell from the rigging to the deck and broke his leg. His father splinted it, and one of the mates made him a cane, and before long he was as good as new.

Whaling inspired plenty of mischief and pranks. One little fellow, only two and a half years old (born on the coast of Chile), was on his way home to New Bedford when he threw the cook's hat overboard and yelled, "There she breaches!" A Nantucket boy was so impressed by his years a-whaling that he tied darning thread to a table fork and harpooned the cat, crying, "Pay out, Mother, there she sounds through the window!"

Seagoing children grew up faster than land children. They soon learned to trust their fathers' skill, to endure dangers without panic, to be considerate of other people in close quarters, to practice tidy shipboard housekeeping, to amuse themselves, not to complain, and to appreciate "little things." They kept diaries, made up games-for-one, and played with dolls and toy boats their skipper-fathers made for them. They visited strange and wonderful ports, and once home in New England with a million tales to tell, they felt quite grand. Whaling children grew up to be captains and captains' wives.

Superstitious sailors considered the birth of a baby on board the luckiest of all omens, but most captains tried to reach port when a baby was expected. One Nantucket wife gave birth to a son on Upolo Island, Samoa, and when he was three weeks old, carried him on board her husband's ship wrapped in banana leaves. Back again in Nantucket, she tried staying home with the baby but found it much too dull, so she took him back to sea as soon as possible. She sailed with her husband thirty-two years in all, and her son

spent his entire boyhood at sea. He took an oar in a whaleboat at twelve and harpooned his first whale at sixteen. He
got married at home at twenty-two and left the next day
on a whaling voyage. In mid-Pacific his ship gammed with
his parents' ship, and he gave them the good news that he
and his sister were both married.

The length of a whaling voyage was more noticeable
when a growing child was on board. Sailors, although
superstitious, seldom minded having a woman on board a
whaleship, and a little girl was better still. Thousands of
miles from his home and family, many a sailor smiled at the
sight of a doll sprawled on the deck of his dingy ship. Captains often drew chalk lines across the deck and told their
children sternly to stay on their own side of the line and not
to associate with the crew. But many a child walked up to
the line and put his toes *exactly* on the edge and peeked at
the sailors, and no foremast hand could resist the adoring
glances of the captain's children, who thought "poor Jack"
was a hero indeed.

Seagoing children stored up vivid memories: eating duff
with raisins or cranberries, steamed in a bag and served
with molasses; or being given a bright green parrot by the
mate after a shore leave; or sitting in a wooden bathtub the
cooper built. One lad remembered watching the poor
greenhands drilling while his mother cut out a new pair of
pants to sew for the cabin boy. A captain's little girl remembered all her life how, when she was five, there were forty
Galápagos tortoises on deck all at once, and how one of the
sailors carved her name on the shell of one of the turtles
and set it free.

Whaling wives took part in gams; they were lowered into
a whaleboat in a special rope-slung chair, to tend the sick or

visit with another woman from home, or gossip and make up a pie or a batch of jelly—in mid-ocean! And children always received little presents, sweets, toys, or cards, from the other captain's wife.

One girl of six and her brother, almost two, sailed on a particularly long and interesting voyage. They slept in their parents' stateroom in two little bunks that were fitted with latticework to keep the children from falling out. Their mother had once been a schoolteacher, and after she taught Laura her lessons in a small schoolroom set up on deck, Laura taught her little brother the alphabet.

Laura loved to dress up and climb on a chair and sing songs to an imaginary audience in the cabin. Her brother played with a pet kitten and hammered away on boards and nails his father, the skipper, had found for him. He had a little rope swing on deck, and the cabin boy liked to play with him and make him laugh. Both children liked to watch the cutting in, and they climbed the transom in the cabin to watch the man-eating sharks that followed the ship.

They were lucky enough to round dread Cape Horn in fair weather, and they marveled at the great black rocks lined with penguins, standing in rows like soldiers. And when they reached Honolulu, after five months at sea, the two-year-old boy screamed and refused to put his foot down on the beach—he had forgotten what land was! He got used to land quickly enough when they all went flower-picking, and he loved to gobble coconut meat. Laura mailed a letter to her grandmother back in Martha's Vineyard, and kept a journal faithfully. She wrote that her father had made a trap and they had caught some mice on board, and that the hens were laying eggs, and that her father had bought them a little black island pig for a pet.

"Honolulu and Diamond Head" by a Chinese artist.
Courtesy, The Mariners Museum, Newport News, Virginia.

Hawaii was crowded with Yankees twice a year: in March, when the whaleships fitted out for Arctic whaling, and again in November when they prepared to chase the sperm whale in warmer seas. Leaky ships were "hove down" for cleaning and repairs, and oil and whalebone were unloaded to be shipped home on merchant vessels. Honolulu, once a tiny native village, had become a New-England-style seaport, with a meetinghouse built of coral blocks, ship chandleries, and shops well stocked with pins and needles, hardware, textiles, and rum. The streets were thronged with resident Yankee traders, missionaries, and boisterous whalers.

Sea captains bound for the Arctic usually left their wives and children in Honolulu and returned for them in the fall. The wives and children loved Hawaii, for they met many friends from home and enjoyed drives in the country, shopping, and band concerts. Many of the wives settled down to await the birth of a new baby. One captain returned from the north to find a darling little daughter, well cared for by native nurses in colorful "Mother Hubbard" dresses. He proudly pronounced the baby "fat as a little pig" but a beauty all the same, and took her aboard his ship, where she slept in a little crib next to her parents' bed.

Sadly, not all babies did as well. One captain, still mourning his first son, who had died while he was away at sea, took his wife and second son with him on his next voyage. Two years out of New Bedford the little boy and his mother landed at Honolulu to wait until her next baby arrived. The captain went on to chase the bowhead whale in the twenty-four-hour daylight of the Arctic summer. In August a girl, named Grace, was born, and in November the whole family sailed for home. The sailors made the baby girl their special pet, but before she was two years old she died, several hundred miles off the coast of Chile. Months later, in the cemetery of the home town that little Grace had never seen, her parents put up a tiny gravestone that read:

Born at the Sandwich Islands
Aug. 9, 1853
Died May 1, 1855, at Sea
in Lat 40 deg S
Lon 78 deg W

About the same time, a pretty sixteen-year-old Australian girl on the way to visit her sister in San Francisco met a young whaling captain from Martha's Vineyard. They fell in love and were married in the seamen's chapel at Honolulu. A few years later they had two daughters, one born at Talcahuano in Chile and the other at Paita in Peru. The little girls were christened in the Catholic cathedral at Paita (although the family were not Catholics themselves), and all the "quality folk" of the seaport and many sea-captain friends attended. The padre spoke in Latin, Spanish, and the local Indian language. As the party left the church the happy father tossed a handful of gold coins to the waiting crowd. (One of his little daughters picked one up and never let it go.) When the sisters arrived home, aged nearly three and nearly two, they astonished the children of Martha's Vineyard by riding around on the back of a giant Galápagos turtle they had brought home from the Pacific.

The sailors' best hope of escaping the confinement of the ship was the liberty stop. Paita and Talcahuano, dusty and sun-drenched, were known as "Sailors' Heaven"—dirty and wicked ports where the captains generally ended up rescuing an entire watch from the local jail, or hunting them up in all the grogshops of the towns.

Honolulu, Lahaina, and Hilo, all in the Sandwich Islands, were favorite stops. Traders and whalers were also fond of the Bay of Islands, New Zealand, with its protected anchorages, good water, and timber, supplied by hustling Maori traders. Tahiti, Samoa, Tonga, and the Society Islands were all pleasant supply ports, and bartering was great sport in the islands. Nothing was so highly prized in some ports as whale's teeth. Island chieftains wore them around their necks as symbols of their rank.

Perhaps the happiest people in the whole South Pacific were the natives of Tonga, or the Friendly Islands. Some sailors and whalers complained that they never could have much fun in the islands because the natives were so religious, but the natives were hospitable and charming. One band of whalers found the people of Vau Vau at a prayer meeting in an open-walled, thatched-roofed chapel enthusiastically singing an English hymn the missionaries had taught them. The women wore calico gowns and the men wore preposterous-looking woolen shirts, jackets, trousers, and seaboots—at ninety degrees in the shade! During the pauses in the service they shed their adored clothes and lay about in the shade, eating green coconut meat and drinking coconut milk.

The captain, meanwhile, had come ashore in a whaleboat loaded with blue and white cotton cloth, axes, muskets and gunpowder, fishhooks, knives, and Jew's harps. The natives soon came forward eagerly with bunches of bananas on their backs and conch shells heaped with eggs. Some balanced shoulder yokes adangle with live chickens, and others strained under two-man poles from which live hogs were suspended, their four feet tied together. The captain bargained by holding up his fingers and pointing—fifty chickens for an axe? a hog for a fishhook and a piece of hoop iron?

One young seaman met a native boy on the beach, and the boy asked him to be his friend and invited him to dine at his house. The sailor was seated in a room furnished only with heaps of leaves arranged on the bare earth floor. The boy's father dug around in the dirt with a huge knife and finally brought up a bundle wrapped in leaves and tied with a vine, as well as a gigantic yam several feet long. He peeled the steaming yam, and its meat was as white as milk. After he placed the yam on a bed of leaves in front of his guest, he undid the bundle. It contained a perfect, tender, juicy chicken, cooked ever so gently for two days over charcoal in a hole covered over with pebbles and earth.

The host flatly refused to join his young guest at the feast. He watched the lad eat, and then, for dessert, he brought out sweet oranges and red bananas with flesh like jelly, and a cornhusk cigarette to top it all off.

In all too short a time, the ship made ready to sail. It looked more like a market boat than a whaleship, with bunches of bananas hung in the rigging, bins of green coconuts on deck, and a cargo of oranges, pineapples, yams, ducks, pigs, and fowls.

The island men were delightedly fingering gifts of whalemen's clothing: knitted socks, ear-flap caps, and even an Arctic ship pilot's suit—of all things! The women unrolled bolts of printed cotton cloth, which was somewhat better suited to the climate. Then, as the ship glided out of the harbor, the natives stood sadly on the beach, waving and crying, "*Ofa, al-ofa, papalang*" ("good-bye, good-bye, white man!").

Many Yankee sailors, desperately sick of life aboard a whaleship, were bewitched by dreams of spending the rest of their lives eating and sleeping, sleeping and eating, living like kings beside the coral sands and turquoise seas, married to some native princess. Yet while many of them deserted to try island life, few stayed for long. They could not get used to the island food, the strange local customs, the idleness, and even the wild life—spiders, scorpions, and giant cockroaches.

One young boatsteerer spent just one afternoon wandering on an island, hunting wild pigeons and listening dreamily to the soft swish of the long combers. He sat down on the root mound of a tall coconut palm and unwrapped his lunch of salt beef and hardtack. Suddenly, not two feet away, he saw a ripe coconut roll over all by itself—and then a forty-pound dry coconut stem rolled over too. When a coconut leaped a foot up into the air, the boy was ready to swim all the way back to Nantucket. He stared in amazement at a fantastic giant crab that was holding a coconut in its claws and trying to pull the husk off.

Islanders' tastes in food were not generally to the liking of Yankees. Doughy pastes made from tropical roots and fruits were a far cry from salt cod and Indian pudding. One captain knew, like most Yankees, that the Hawaiians raised both pigs and dogs for meat, but he steadfastly refused to eat dog. He was invited with several other skippers to an island barbecue, and was particularly pleased with a delectable country-style "baked pig" that was served. Only it wasn't pig, and when he found out, he swore off Polynesian feasts for several years.

But for provisions, brief stops at the islands were quite necessary and pleasant. Afterward, there were as many as ten or twenty hogs running around the deck up forward, not to mention hundreds of fowls, loose or in coops. The hogs were forever getting tangled up in the men's legs. The men cursed and kicked as the hogs slid back and forth across the rolling deck. The poor animals could never learn to stay put once they slid across, but dug their toes into the slanting timbers and struggled up to windward again, grunting and bracing their feet. Up rose the ship, and over rolled the hogs! Once in a while a terrified pig would sail overboard, and the men just lowered a whaleboat and fished him out again. Pigs, in fact, were very good sailors.

Sailing in the vast Pacific held terrors for whalemen as well as pleasures though. A sickening feeling of unknown danger gripped the men when the wind died and they drifted with the current in an uncharted sea toward a strange island. They well knew that on some islands savage cannibals waited for ships to run aground on submerged reefs and then rushed on board to murder the crew and plunder the vessel. When whalemen spotted charred ship's timbers in unfamiliar waters, their bones grew cold, for the savages were known to set fire to plundered hulks and leave them on the reefs until the waves and surf broke up the remains.

When captains held Sabbath services on deck in these waters, they noticed that even the roughest of the seamen were moving their lips in prayer, fearful of sudden attack, forced tattooing and slavery, or torture and violent death.

Few calls were ever made at the dread islands of Melanesia, home of giant cannibals who pursued strange vessels in two-hundred-man war canoes with huge sails of palm-leaf matting. The warriors remained absolutely silent at first and then suddenly paralyzed the sailors with blood-curdling war cries. Armed with swords made of rows of sharks' teeth set in coconut bark, scores of natives would swarm up the sides of a whaleship. Some thirty whalemen had to defend themselves at the rail, swinging lances and cutting spades. Their only chance of escaping with their lives rested on the hope of wounding or disgracing the chief.

Fiji Islanders were known to set up great stone baking ovens in sacred groves by the beach, where they roasted human beings in their religious ceremonies. They called the meat "long pig," and the ovens, dishes, and long wooden forks they used were "taboo" for any other purpose.

Yet these same Fiji natives could behave in baffling ways. There was one young and powerful king who presented a whaling captain with a cow. In a few days the fat, arrogant chief was invited on board ship for a meal. When the steward offered him a bowl of beef soup, the cannibal king dramatically refused to taste it. He explained that the cow had been born on his island. He could still picture her grazing contentedly, and he loved her, and so he could not possibly *eat* her!

Months and years passed by while a whaleship sailed back and forth across the wide Pacific. Then one day, almost incredibly, every cask was full of oil. The mate called all hands to get the ship under way for home. The men were so excited that they had all sails set by the time the anchor was up. The grimy vessel began to lumber away to make the passage round the Horn, her bottom covered with barnacles, and dragging a yard of weeds from her hull.

Our yards we'll swing and our sails we'll set,
  Good-bye, fare ye well,
  Good-bye, fare ye well:
The whales we are leaving, we leave with regret,
  Hurrah, my bullies, we're homeward bound!

On the long homeward passage the men tarred down the rigging, scraped and painted the spars, masts, and wood-work, and painted the hull down to the waterline. They took up the boats, dismantled the lookouts, and broke up the brick-and-mortar tryworks and threw it overboard. Then they stowed their gear, got out their shore clothes, and whiled away the hours scrimshawing. One day they sighted a patch of seaweed in the ocean—a sign that they were in the warmer waters of the Gulf Stream, off the east coast of North America.

A few days later they "spoke" a small Cape Cod schooner and got some fresh fish to eat. After four years away, nothing was so disappointing as a rain squall or heavy fog that hid the first sight of land—Block Island, perhaps, or Montauk Point. But when the weather was clear, even the watch below raced up on deck to catch a glimpse of home— "Clark's Point Light open on our port bow!" The crew stood and gazed at the land in silence, while the officers earnestly discussed the price of oil. Before long, the pilot came on board to guide the ship into New Bedford.

One ship dropped anchor in the lower harbor just as the nine o'clock bells rang out from the old stone church. The mate and several of the others rowed ashore to make the ship's safe arrival known, and the vessel came all the way in before midnight. Friends and relatives waited on the wharf, and clothing outfitters even came on board to take measurements, and returned with new clothes for the patchy whalers.

Then the men and boys went their separate ways, with hardly a backward glance at the fellows with whom they had shared close quarters, boredom, tension, and danger for four long years. The lads and drifters with nowhere to go were taken in tow by the same waterfront "sharks" who had packed them off to sea.

The oil casks were hoisted from the hold and placed in long rows on the wharf, and the gauger made ready to measure the contents of each with a long rod. The ship was hove down on its side to be scraped and cleaned and checked for decaying timbers. The hull was then caulked with oakum and pitch or sheathed in copper plate. Before long it was made ready and fitted out for its next long journey—"bound to any ocean."

"Clark's Point Light, New Bedford" by William Bradford.
The Whaling Museum, New Bedford.

THE END OF THE STORY

WHEN GOLD WAS DISCOVERED in California in 1848, many people in the East took the news with disbelief. Then gold nuggets began to arrive in New England along with glowing reports of the fortunes to be made in the hills of the West. Gold fever swept the country—no town escaped the madness—and the rush of the Forty-Niners was on, to the rollicking tune of "Oh, Susanna."

> Oh, California! That's the land for me!
> I'm going to Sacramento with my washbowl on my knee!

Just a few years before, in 1846, a terrible fire had destroyed a third of the business center of Nantucket, including the waterfront area. The islanders, stunned at their million-dollar loss, never recovered their bold spirit. In New Bedford, meanwhile, some of the wealthy men, who had been accustomed to invest their money in whaling, were using their whale-oil fortunes to support new cotton textile mills in hopes of more certain profits.

Whaleships would still be leaving New England ports for many years—New Londoners chased the right whale in the South Indian Ocean, and Arctic whaling grew very active. All the same, many men began signing on Pacific whaleships just to get a free ride to California. They deserted immediately upon landing. Entire crews, their captains and officers with them, walked off their ships to go prospecting, and the harbor of San Francisco was soon jammed with abandoned vessels.

The ramshackle town swarmed with adventurers, and for a couple of years all goods were in short supply. Some men

"California News" by William S. Mount. *Courtesy of the Suffolk Museum & Carriage House at Stony Brook, Long Island, New York.*

made the fortune of a lifetime overnight simply by being able to offer a cargo of New England potatoes at sixteen dollars a bushel or a load of eggs that had been all the way around Cape Horn at ten dollars a dozen. Tacks, shoes, wooden pilings, dry goods—these, even more than gold, meant instant success to those who had shiploads of them to sell in San Francisco.

Speed became a passion—speed to 'Frisco for gold and speed to the Orient for profits in trade. The Yankee clipper ships of the 1850s, carrying almost incredibly tall clouds of square white sails, thrilled the world. Fast and smart, the clippers were commanded by hard-driving, highly paid captains, many of them from Cape Cod, men who would do anything to break a speed record. Several clippers, their sails shredding and their lee rails under water, made the trip from New York to San Francisco in eighty-nine days, and no other sailing ships have *ever* beaten that record.

The costly and beautiful clippers were supreme among sailing ships, with their smooth black hulls, creamy white decks, rails of polished brass and rosewood, and luxurious passenger cabins. But the clipper-ship years were years of shame as well as glory. More seamen were needed than ever

Ship card, *Susan Fearing.*
Courtesy of The New-York Historical Society, New York City.

before, but the work was hard and dangerous and the pay was miserable. Foremast hands, under the rule of brutal officers, were little more than slaves.

Self-respecting boys shunned the clippers just as they shunned the whaleships. They took promising and well-paid jobs in the factories, or turned to the rich and fertile farm-lands of the Middle West. Yankee lads who could not over-come their sea fever worked in the Grand Banks fisheries, perhaps, or chose the fair pay and good working conditions on the coasters.

No one could possibly know that a new kind of oil—petroleum—would be discovered in Pennsylvania in 1859. And few people could foresee that two years after that, a great civil war was to tear the struggling young nation apart, and all but destroy its fleet of whaleships and mer-chant ships.

The great days of American sailing and whaling were past. Proud Yankee "Jack," who had won over the world with his skill and daring, his engaging manner, his style, and his youth, was not seen again.

Oh around the corner we will go,
Round the corner Sally!

We'd like to stay but we've got to go,
Round the corner Sally!

Glossary

able seaman — a skilled, experienced seaman

bark — a three-masted vessel with foremast and mainmast square-rigged and mizzenmast fore-and-aft rigged

barrel — a measure for liquids, equal to 31½ gallons

block and tackle — a set of pulleys and ropes for hoisting

blubber — the fat of whales and other marine mammals

boatsteerer — harpooner (a whaleman's term)

boom — a spar used to stretch the bottom of a fore-and-aft sail

bow — the front or "forward" end of a vessel

brig — a two-masted, square-rigged vessel

cask — a barrel-shaped wooden container, usually for liquids

caulk — to drive fibers, such as oakum, into cracks between the wood planks of a vessel, to prevent leaks

chandlery — a shop dealing in small wares and provisions

cooper — a maker or repairer of casks and barrels

counting house — the business office of a merchant or trader

dead reckoning—finding the position of a ship from the record of courses followed and the distances sailed on each, without the help of celestial observations.

dory — a flat-bottomed rowboat with flaring sides

dray — a low wagon without permanent sides, for heavy loads

duff — a stiff flour pudding, boiled in a bag

ensign — a banner or flag

fathom — a measure of length or depth, equal to six feet

flukes — a whale's powerful tail

fore-and-aft-rigged — fitted with triangular or rectangular sails carried in a front-to-back direction

forecastle (fo'c'sle) — the crew's quarters, in the bow

furl — to wrap or roll tightly

galley — the cooking area of a vessel

gam — a social visit between whaleships at sea

greenhand — an inexperienced hand on his first whaling voyage grog — a mixed drink, usually rum and water

hardtack — sea bread; hard biscuit

harpoon — a barbed spear used to strike whales or large fish

heave to — to bring a vessel to a standstill

hemp — the tough fibers of an Asian plant; used in ropemaking

hogshead — a measure for liquids, equal to 63 gallons

hold — the interior of a vessel, below the lower deck, where the cargo is stowed

"the Horn" — Cape Horn

hull — the body or frame of a vessel

Kanaka — a native of the South Pacific; often, a Hawaiian

larboard — an old term that meant the same as "port"

lay — a share of the profits, especially on whaling voyages

leeward—the direction towards which the wind is blowing; the lee side of a vessel is sheltered from the wind

"the Line" — the Equator

mast — a long, round, upright timber to which yards, rigging, and sails are fastened

mate — a deck officer ranking below the captain

mizzenmast — the rearmost mast on a three-masted vessel

monsoon — a seasonal wind of south Asia

oakum — loose fibers obtained from picking and untwisting old ropes

pilot — a man qualified to escort vessels in and out of a harbor

port — looking toward the bow, the left-hand side of a vessel

quintal — a measure for split and salted fish; a European hundred-weight, equal to about 220 pounds

rigging — all the ropes and chains that raise and lower or support the masts and spars and set the sails

right whale — a toothless, two-spouted mammal of temperate and Arctic seas, hunted for whalebone and oil

schooner — a fore-and-aft-rigged vessel with two or more masts

scrimshaw — polished and decorated ivory articles made by American seamen from the teeth of sperm whales

scurvy — a painful disease caused by a lack of vitamin C (fresh fruits and vegetables) on long voyages ship — any large vessel; specifically, a large square-rigged vessel that generally has three masts, all of which are made up of several sections, and is fitted with a full array of sails

sloop — a fore-and-aft-rigged vessel with one mast

soundings — measurements of the depth and composition of the ocean floor, taken by means of a line weighted with a piece of lead

spar — a round or oval timber such as a mast, yard, or boom

sperm whale — a huge toothed mammal of warm oceans, hunted for sperm oil and other valuable substances; it has a single blowhole connected to its windpipe

square-rigged — having principal sails extended on yards that are hung horizontally across the vessel from side to side

starboard — looking toward the bow, the right-hand side of a vessel

stern — the rear or "after" end of a vessel

supercargo — the merchant's or shipowner's representative on a trading voyage; in charge of commercial matters, not navigation

tallow — the fat of sheep or oxen

tamarind — the datelike pod of a tropical tree; used in preserves

try out — to refine fat by melting it; on a whaleship, to boil cut-up pieces of blubber in try-pots on deck

watch — a period of time, usually four hours, when a seaman is assigned to duty on deck; also, the group of officers and crewmen who together run the vessel during that time

windward — the direction from which the wind is blowing

yard — a long, tapered spar fitted crosswise to a mast to support a square sail

yarn — an adventure story, not always strictly truthful

Suggested Further Reading

HERE is an informal list of books that should interest readers who have enjoyed *Blow Ye Winds Westerly*. First, four great nineteenth-century classics:

Moby Dick, or The White Whale by Herman Melville. Surely the greatest book about whaling ever written, by a man who shipped aboard a whaleship bound for the South Pacific when he was twenty-one, *Moby Dick* is the story of the men of the *Pequod* and their maimed captain's relentless pursuit of the malevolent white whale. (The novel contains a great deal of background material about whales and whaling, and younger readers might like to start with an abridged version.)

Two Years Before the Mast by Richard Henry Dana. A Harvard student interrupts his education and sails as a foremast hand on a voyage around Cape Horn to California. (Young Dana very nearly gave in to the lure of the sea for good, but returned to become a lawyer and devote the rest of his life to the cause of sailors' rights to better living conditions and to just and fair treatment by ships' officers and courts.)

The House of the Seven Gables by Nathaniel Hawthorne. This is the gentle yet suspenseful tale of the impoverished descendants of a once powerful family of Salem, living under the shadow of a curse that goes back to the days of terror and witchcraft in the late 1600s.

Captains Courageous by Robert Louis Stevenson. This exciting, fast-moving book tells of the coming-of-age of a pampered lad who falls overboard from an ocean liner and is picked up by a band of fishermen out of Gloucester. He has no choice but to share the rugged life of his rescuers on a Banks schooner, and by the time he eventually returns with them to port, he is a wiser, more understanding young man.

Now, some books for readers with special interests:

Johnny Tremain by Esther Forbes. A silversmith's apprentice experiences personal pain and misfortune and is caught up in the first exhilarating events that lead up to the War of Independence, including the Boston Tea Party. (Houghton Mifflin Co., 1943; Dell Yearling paperback.)

Sailing the Seven Seas by Mary Ellen Chase. A member of an old Maine family writes about family life at sea, as well as some incredible adventures. (Houghton Mifflin Co., 1958; Dell Yearling paperback.)

A New England Boyhood by Edward Everett Hale. These are the cheerful recollections of a well-to-do Boston boy, born in 1822, about his home life, games, holidays, excursions, school, and his entrance to college at the age of thirteen. (Little, Brown paperback.)

Memories of Old Salem by Mary Harrod Northend. Drawn from the letters of a great-grandmother, here are memories of daily life, school, clothes, parties—and the tragic romance of a Salem girl, waiting in the family mansion, and a young man who sailed away, never to return. (Moffatt, Yard & Co., 1917.)

The Story of a Bad Boy by Thomas Bailey Aldrich. Lots of mischief and high spirits infect this funny, heartwarming memoir (first published in 1870) of a boy growing up in a seaport very much like Portsmouth, New Hampshire. (Pantheon, 1951.)

Nightbirds on Nantucket by Joan Aiken. Two girls, one bold and one timid, become entangled in a mystery that begins on a whaleship and deepens in the cottages and on the windswept moors of the island. (Doubleday, 1966; Dell Yearling paperback.)

Whaling Wives by Emma Mayhew Whiting and Henry Beetle Hough. Here are true adventures in the lives of captains' wives and children from Martha's Vineyard on voyages in the Pacific and Arctic oceans. (Houghton Mifflin Co., 1952.)

The Year of the Whale by Victor B. Scheffer. This is a beautiful account of the birth and first year of a baby whale, portraying the intelligence and loyalty of a remarkable mammal that has been too little respected by man. (Scribner, 1969; Scribner paperback.)

Little Calf by Victor B. Scheffer. An adaptation of *The Year of the Whale* for readers 8 to 12 years old. (Scribner, 1970.)

MYSTIC SEAPORT, a few miles east of New London, Connecticut, is a reconstructed nineteenth-century village at the water's edge. There are dwellings, a schoolhouse, chapel, general store, tavern, clock shop with nautical instruments, apothecary shop and doctor's office, cooperage, ropewalk, shipsmith's shop and forge, sail loft, ship chandlery, counting house, and museum buildings that display figureheads, scrimshaw, ship models, paintings, and much, much more. Best of all, there are several real vessels to explore above and below decks—the *L. A. Dunton*, a sturdy Gloucester fishing schooner, and the *Charles W. Morgan*, last wooden whaleship in the world, are especially popular.

Index

(Page numbers in italic indicate illustrations.)

About the Author

Elizabeth Gemming is a descendant of the earliest settlers of New England, and has spent part of each summer at the family homestead in New Hampshire. Her first book for young readers was HUCKLEBERRY HILL, an affectionate recreation of New England country life in the early nineteenth century.

Mrs. Gemming was graduated from Wellesley College, and has studied and taught in Germany on a Fulbright scholarship. She has worked as an editor and translator, and with her husband, the distinguished book designer Klaus Gemming, has written several books for children. The Gemmings and their two daughters live in New Haven, Connecticut.